Social Work Using Interpretative Phenomenological Analysis

Social Work Using Interpretative Phenomenological Analysis

A Methodological Approach for Practice and Research

Sarah Vicary and Gillian Ferguson

Open University Press

Open University Press
McGraw Hill
Unit 4
Foundation Park
Roxborough Way
Maidenhead
SL6 3UD

email: emea_uk_ireland@mheducation.com
world wide web: www.mheducation.co.uk

Executive Editor: Sam Crowe
Editorial Assistant: Hannah Jones
Content Product Manager: Graham Jones

British Library Cataloguing in Publication Data
A catalogue record of this book is available from the British Library

ISBN-13: 978-0-3352-5236-7
ISBN-10: 0335252362
eISBN: 978-0-3352-5237-4

Typeset by Transforma Pvt. Ltd., Chennai, India

Praise page

"This book is a welcome addition to the small but growing corpus of knowledge surrounding Interpretative Phenomenological Analysis (IPA) and social work research. The inclusion of the authors' doctoral studies gives the book a unique and practical perspective. It positions social work firmly within the qualitative research paradigm and makes a convincing argument about the 'fit' between IPA and the profession. This book should be read by research students, early career researchers, social work practitioners as well as doctoral supervisors new to IPA, who will all find it helpful and insightful."

Dr Angie Bartoli, School of Social Sciences Student Experience Manager,
Principal Lecturer in Social Work, Nottingham Trent University, UK

"Firmly grounded in the authors' own research experience, this accessible text successfully explores the developing relationship between IPA and social work, locating IPA firmly in the broader landscape of social work research. It will be an extremely helpful companion to social work researchers at all stages of the research process from design though to dissemination, as well of being of real value to those supervising IPA projects."

Dr Martin Kettle, Senior Lecturer,
Glasgow Caledonian University, UK

"This much needed and timely book is sure to be a go-to text for anybody interested in using IPA to explore social work. The use of the authors' doctoral studies to provide examples throughout the book make it easy to move from theory to really understanding the application of these concepts. Doctoral supervisors and academics will benefit from this accessible and engaging book as much as researchers thinking of using IPA in their studies."

Lindsay Giddings, Lecturer in Social Work and Programme Lead for
Undergraduate and Apprenticeship Social Work, The Open University

Contents

Foreword

As the Editor of the Sage journal, *Qualitative Social Work*, I have been looking for a book like this for many years. We are seeing an increase in submissions which claim to use Interpretative Phenomenological Analysis (IPA); however, we often find they are only engaging in certain aspects of the theoretical underpinnings. I have never used IPA which has meant that as an editor, I have looked to the expertise of those who, like the authors, have both used and understand this approach. Having read the book, I now feel confident that I could review an IPA article. I had never really understood what the 'double hermeneutic' is, but I do now because the authors describe it in such an engaging and clear way. Previously, I have also never understood how Husserl differs from Heidegger – but again now I do!

Aimed at social workers (and adjacent professionals) who are considering using IPA in their research, this book will also be invaluable to doctoral students and other more established researchers. It is an in-depth comprehensive guide which reflects the authoritative knowledge of the authors, but it is not hard to follow. This is a reflection on how well the authors understand IPA and their commitment to supporting other researchers to use IPA in their own research. The writing style is highly engaging. It is written with clarity and with the reader in mind. The pedagogical approach is excellent. I particularly love the authors' conversations and examples, including the extracts from their research journals. These vitalise the approach, making it feel more 'real' and concrete and lift the book from a usual textbook. This makes you feel that the authors have been where the reader is, grappling with the same issues and decisions the reader will be having as part of their own doctoral journey.

The topics that the book covers build on one another in a highly skilful way, beginning with an understanding of the theoretical underpinnings of IPA. It then moves on to all the different elements of using IPA in research. The authors make it clear how IPA differs from the other research approaches which a researcher might be considering (Grounded Theory, Ethnomethodology, Narrative, and Action Research). This will be extremely helpful for researchers new to social work research to develop an understanding of exactly what each approach offers – and where IPA is situated in this space. Chapter 3 of the book switches to the practicalities of undertaking IPA research, introducing an integrated holistic model. The model represented in Figure 3.1 is excellent in combining all the different elements and enables the reader to fully gain an understanding of the IPA approach.

Part 2 of the book carefully goes through all the different elements, from the design choices which are vital, to the sample research site and data collection in Chapter 4. Chapter 5 is devoted to making sense of the material, showing how analysis is at the heart of IPA research. Again, I loved reading the examples from both authors' doctoral journeys on delving into the data. It was excellent to see how Sarah used NVivo, and how Gillian moved from initial noting to disciplined notes and then seeing the whole pinned to the wall. IPA research needs to include a focus on idiography, phenomenology and the sense-making double hermeneutic process. In my experience, and as the authors note, the latter is often neglected. Chapter 6 discusses how to represent these complex and multi-layered findings. This is not an easy stage for novice researchers. Through using their own examples, the authors actively demonstrate how they individually accomplished this. I really like Figures 6.1 and 6.3 on how Gillian interpreted her analysis of the lived experience of her participants.

The chapter on supervision is such an important addition, especially as doctoral students are likely to have a supervisor who is not *au fait* with IPA. It opens the book to another set of readers: doctoral supervisors. Again, it is comprehensive, taking the reader through all the different elements, from the design, the doing and the defence.

Part 3 of the book has many important elements – such as dealing with areas that might come up in a viva, including sample size and generalisability – which are not the focus of IPA research as such given that its aim is to explore the ideographic or lived experience. I like how the authors include the limitations of IPA here too; namely, that there is a sense that it is more psychological than social. They consider how the social might be incorporated in future directions of IPA in the conclusion.

This is such an excellent book. I have taught research methods for over 10 years, and this exceeds all the books on social work research that I have used to date. This book feels warm, encouraging and collegiate. It is a must-read for anyone interested in using IPA in social work research.

Lisa Morriss
Editor: *Qualitative Social Work*

Acknowledgements

The book is dedicated to the authors' respective doctoral supervisors, who supported their early journeys with IPA, and all the extraordinary social workers engaged in daily practice.

Professor Alys Young, Dr Stephen Hicks (Sarah), Dr Mark Wareing and Professor Jan Draper (Gillian) – we thank you.

Introduction

Welcome to *Social Work Using Interpretative Phenomenological Analysis: A Methodological Approach for Practice and Research*. This book aims to explore the theoretical foundations alongside the practical aspects of undertaking an IPA study related to social work research and practice. Interpretative Phenomenological Analysis (IPA) was first introduced in an article by Jonathan Smith in which he discusses its origin and its suggested place in health psychology (Smith 1996). Many developments have taken place since that seminal publication, culminating in what has become a ground-breaking methodological approach which is described in two editions of an academic textbook by Smith and other proponents (Smith et al. 2009 and 2022). Albeit a relatively new methodology in the qualitative research tradition, IPA now forms the methodological basis of research in many discipline areas, and this is increasingly so in social work. This book is written for people considering IPA from different perspectives, including: social work students; social work practitioners; doctoral students; research supervisors; and anyone else who is interested! The book will guide readers through its application in this field.

Divided into three parts, the first outlines the interface between qualitative social work research, IPA, social work practice and social work research. Its first two chapters outline IPA through its main theoretical and conceptual underpinnings and its relevance as a qualitative research methodology into social work professional practice. According to its developers and proponents, IPA is a study of experience guided by three theoretical influences: phenomenology, hermeneutics and idiography (Smith 2004, 2007; Reid et al. 2005; Larkin et al. 2006; Smith et al. 2009; Shinebourne 2011). The book will discuss each of these influences and examine what is meant by experience. Based on an interpretative paradigm, IPA draws upon a range of influences. From an ontological perspective, IPA focuses on subjective reality and does so from the viewpoint of the participant. Epistemologically, knowledge arises from the meaning the participant makes of their experience, or reality. IPA encourages the acquisition of knowledge through exploring meaning and sense-making, by the participant and by the researcher. Key theoretical influences drive IPA: adopting the phenomenological attitude, engaging in the hermeneutic circle and focusing on a particular phenomenon. Part 1 concludes with Chapter 3 setting out the necessary ethical foundations and focus of an effective study. We consider the connection between your role as a researcher or supervisor, interests and perspectives, along with the importance of an effective support network. The book introduces a holistic model for IPA in social work research that provides a framework for designing, undertaking, supervising and reviewing a study. Using our own experiences of undertaking qualitative research to provide evidence for social work practice, we argue that research using IPA is a good fit, the doing of which you will consider in more depth in Part 2.

Part 2 continues taking the reader on a journey through designing and doing an effective IPA study using the components of the holistic model as a guide. In Chapter 4 we consider appropriate methods for IPA social work research building on ethical foundations. A detailed discussion about how to maximise the skills of data collection to elicit rich and detailed phenomenological data is central to the chapter. Weaving the integrated elements of IPA throughout an effective research project is a guiding principle with attention to the details in the research design, methods and procedures essential to generate the kind of data needed. Chapter 5 shifts to thinking about the complexity of analysis in IPA studies, linking with the integrated model and providing a pathway to arrive at interpreted accounts of lived experience. Analysis is central to any research project and the book positions this as an immersive hermeneutic sense-making quest. Your role as researcher is central to this process as you delve into the data. The chapter explores how to confidently work towards clear findings before moving into a detailed discussion in Chapter 6 about how to represent these creatively. The discussion focuses on representing findings that stay true to the essence of lived experience, remain respectful to the people who have participated and that you can communicate to different audiences. How any new knowledge generated through research feeds into the existing literature and broader knowledge landscape remains important. The possibilities for influence and impact are intricately linked with how your findings are communicated. Making a difference in social work through IPA research is therefore a strong thread of the discussion as Chapter 6 concludes.

Readers may be involved in diverse types of research project and having an effective network that guides a study is introduced early in the book. Chapter 7 moves to focus on the nature of formal research supervision for IPA research in social work. Beginning with an overview of the purpose of supervision in social work, the discussion primarily speaks to supervisors and supervisees in relation to developing an effective working alliance. It considers the specific issues of guiding IPA studies through their design, and the doing and defence of them. This includes how supervisors or doctoral students who are not from a social work background grapple with the professional issues inherent in any study.

Part 3 of the book returns to thinking about the broad landscape of IPA as a potential for action and change in the social work field. It consists of Chapter 8, which provides a summary view to the horizon of IPA in social work, returning to the current literature, examples and opportunities of the approach. Some suggestions are also made for future developments before our conclusions are reached.

Motivation for the book stems from our experiences as doctoral students, academic researchers, academic and practice supervisors and also as social workers, with both of us having worked in different practice and leadership roles. We both remain close to direct practice. A chance conversation led to the discovery of a shared passion for the philosophical underpinnings and potential of IPA for social work. We also encountered regular queries about IPA as academic reviewers and research supervisors. Study examples, regularly encountered, had the integrated elements only partially considered. The intention in this book is to develop a clear guide, specific to social work that draws from our own and others' experiences.

The book is written in a conversational tone and uses examples from two doctoral studies undertaken by the authors to illustrate key points about the methodology. We are clear that we do not offer these as exemplars, but to promote reflection on different approaches so that you can make the choices that are right for your own study. The book does not attempt to cover or reiterate the details of the overarching IPA texts by Jonathan Smith, Michael Larkin and Paul Flowers. Indeed, we recommend readers to refer to these works directly and offer a list of further reading at the end of the book. There is also a plethora of other phenomenological research theory and guidance available. Doctoral students will need to draw from a broad spectrum of underpinning material as they develop plans for their research, and an understanding of the potential and criticism of IPA is essential. Nonetheless, this book provides a dialogue about the practicalities of undertaking an IPA study and a specific focus on the context of social work. The book also offers helpful insights for supervisors and alignment with the context of social work education and continuing professional learning. We hope you enjoy exploring this journey with us.

Part **1**

Discovering Lived Experience Through IPA Social Work Research

Part 1

1 The theory of IPA in qualitative research

Chapter aims:

- to discuss the inception of IPA according to its proponents and developers
- to situate IPA as a research methodology within the qualitative research paradigm
- to outline IPA's three theoretical influences
- to examine the concept of lived experience and its relevance for social work research.

Introduction

In this chapter we provide a summary of the main underpinning theoretical and conceptual bases of IPA, a relatively new research methodology first introduced in a seminal paper in the 1990s (Smith 1996). IPA has undergone much impetus since its inception in health psychology and is now increasingly used in other research and practice or professional disciplines, including social work. While not mentioning social work specifically, van Manen notes that 'that many professions seem to require not only trainable skills and specialised bodies of knowledge but also abilities that have to do with discretionary, intuitive, pathic and tactful capacities' (van Manen 2016: xviii). He suggests that phenomenological research contributes to this. Although initially its theoretical stature was questioned, IPA is now considered to be guided by three theoretical influences: phenomenology, hermeneutics and idiography (Shinebourne 2011). In short, as a methodological approach in the qualitative research tradition, IPA claims to understand, give voice to and make meaning of a phenomenon or person in context (Larkin et al. 2006). Fundamental to IPA is the exploration of the lived experience from the perspective of the person who is deemed an expert in their own experience (Reid et al. 2005). IPA now boasts two textbooks (Smith et al. 2009 and 2022) and attracts much reflection as to its use and the way in which it is developing (Smith 2004; Smith 2007; Smith 2011a; Smith 2011b). This chapter will discuss each underpinning theoretical and conceptual base and will explore in more detail what is meant by lived experience. To begin, however, the ontological and epistemological positioning of IPA is explained. Some of what follows is taken from Sarah's thesis (Vicary 2017: 67–75). The specific location is referenced for ease.

Ontological and epistemological positioning

Meaning making and the double hermeneutic

From an ontological perspective, IPA focuses on subjective reality and does so from the viewpoint of the person. Understanding and making sense – especially about a person's lived experience – underpins IPA, and this is clearly laid out in each textbook (Smith et al. 2009: 1; Smith et al. 2022: 1). These aspects are also endorsed by Larkin and colleagues who earlier proposed two epistemological aspects of IPA: to understand or give voice and to make sense (Larkin et al. 2006). As such, this methodological approach adopts an interpretative ontological stance; that is, it attempts to uncover the nature and meaning of the reality of people's experiences in the world or, to be more precise, the social world. Through its use, the researcher is trying to get to the structure and texture of lived experience and the meaning of this for the person. IPA does not view reality as objective nor is it a positivist research approach since it does not attempt to define the truth or indeed obtain facts. Rather, it seeks to understand and explicate the person's own experience, the meaning they make of it and, crucially, the interpretation which the researcher makes of the person's meaning (Vicary 2017: 67).

Similarly, IPA's epistemological stance rests on the person's subjective account. For IPA's proponents, knowledge arises from the meaning the person makes of their experience or reality. This methodological approach therefore encourages the acquisition of knowledge through meaning-making, by the person and by the researcher. Through the theory of interpretation and the assertion that there are two aspects to meaning-making, protagonists of IPA refer to the process of the researcher making sense of the person's meaning-making as the double hermeneutic (Smith and Osborn 2003). The primary concern of IPA is the lived experience of the person and the meaning they make of it. The result of any exploration is the account of how the researcher thinks the person is thinking (Smith et al. 2009: 80; Smith et al. 2022: 29). An additional step, referred to as the triple hermeneutic, involves the reader making sense of the researcher making sense (Smith et al. 2009: 41; Smith et al. 2022: 36). Additionally, knowledge comes about through understanding which arises through empathy, but also through questioning, a process we will refer to in Part 2 as the researcher's sense-making quest. This dual approach to sense-making is the second meaning of the concept of the double hermeneutic (Vicary 2017: 67).

Aside from the underpinning ontology and epistemology, a range of theoretical stances support IPA. It is important for you to be aware of and understand these influences, both in fathoming how to implement the methodology and in defending its use. These influences are as follows: phenomenology or adopting the phenomenological attitude or bracketing; interpretation or engaging in the hermeneutic circle; and idiography or focusing on a particular phenomenon. We will now consider these influences in the next section of this chapter.

Theoretical influences

Phenomenology, attitude and bracketing

Situated within a continuum which has description at its one end and inter-pretation at its other, IPA adopts an interpretative phenomenological stance. Phenomenology has been described as a shorthand term which refers to both a philosophical movement and a range of research methods (Finlay 2008: 1), both of which are centred on the lived experience. Inaugurated in the early twentieth century by Husserl, the philosophy of phenomenology is concerned with the study of conscious experience of which there are two strands. In the first, descriptive or transcendental phenomenology, the person is said to engage with and make sense of phenomena, sometimes referred to as the natural or taken for granted attitude. This natural attitude is said to be a person's every-day assumptions about how things are. For Husserl, it is possible to get to the essence of a phenomenon by putting aside this natural attitude, a process referred to as the phenomenological reduction. IPA purports that to understand the essence of phenomena as experienced by an individual, the researcher must actively put to one side their natural attitude – a process known as adopting the phenomenological attitude or bracketing. For Husserl, bracketing concerns putting aside the natural world and the world of interpretation to see the phenomenon in its essence (Gil-Rodriguez and Hefferon 2012; Vicary 2017: 68).

The concept and process of bracketing, or adopting the phenomenological attitude, has been challenged not least by those who contend that such reduction is not possible. It is suggested that the best that can be achieved is interpreta-tion, the second phenomenological strand of IPA known as hermeneutic or interpretative phenomenology, and is a version which views individuals and the world as a reciprocal relationship in which both exist and are mutually understood. Consequently, advocates of this second strand contend that the best understanding of a phenomenon achievable is by interpretation only. In other words, meaning for the individual will always be influenced by the external world and will always be subject to previous or fore-understandings. Heidegger, the main proponent of hermeneutic phenomenology, does not accept that adopting the phenomenological attitude, as Husserl proposes, is possible (Heidegger 1962). Heidegger views phenomenology as an interpretative activ-ity shifting beyond description or capture of lived experience.

Bracketing is an important concept in IPA (Dahlberg et al. 2008; Smith et al. 2009; Vicary 2017: 69–70). It refers to the process whereby the researcher attempts to put to one side their own pre-existing historical, cultural and theo-retical knowledge. Another term for actively suspending preconceptions is bridling. IPA uses suspension of preconceptions in two ways: in the sense of phenomenological reduction where the researcher accepts that a person's sub-jective experience exists and that they are trying to get to the essence of it by bracketing the natural attitude; second, in the sense of deliberately putting aside previous knowledge to enable the researcher to understand the essence of the phenomenon. This dual purpose of bracketing causes consternation among some phenomenologists who argue that phenomenological reduction, as it is used here, does not refer to the natural attitude and putting aside preconceptions relies on reflection rather than assuming the attitude of the phenomenological reduction (Giorgi 2010). Apologists for IPA, however, argue the methodology merely borrows from the tradition (Smith 2010). In short, IPA conflates the two understandings of bracketing or bridling and translates the process as follows: one that involves the researcher adopting an open, non-judgemental approach while at the same time being conscious of and holding back past or prior assumptions and understandings or knowledge (Vicary 2017: 69–70).

Interpretation and the hermeneutic circle

Interpretation, or hermeneutics, is a separate underpinning theory of IPA which influences the dynamics of the research and the role of the researcher. Originally, hermeneutics concerned the interpretation of Biblical text and is defined as the attempt to uncover the text's original meaning. As such hermeneutics combines linguistic and psychological elements, namely a focus on what the text denotes and what its author proposed. Hermeneutics links with phenomenology through a component of the philosophy of Heidegger which argues that there will be clues in the text which are integrally connected to that which might otherwise be latent or not overtly present. As such, the role of the researcher is crucial as it helps them to facilitate the showing of the phenomenon and allow meaning, which is otherwise hidden, to appear. In analysing text in detail, IPA borrows the concept of hermeneutics and in doing so proposes that meaning which lies dormant can be unearthed, whether the person who is making sense of the phenomenon is conscious of this or not (Vicary 2017: 70). The need to audit how such unearthing is achieved constitutes the second criterion for measuring the quality of an IPA study and will be discussed in more detail in Part 2 of this book. IPA also deploys interpretation in its suggestion that there is a perspective on the text, or, in research terms data, which arises through detailed and systematic analysis. Consequently, insights which exceed and subsume the explicit claims of the person arise (Smith et al. 2009: 23; Smith et al. 2022: 30). In IPA then, the researcher is inextricably linked with uncovering meaning while also making sense of it. In short, the phenomenon cannot be known without the interpretation.

A further concept of central importance to IPA is the hermeneutic or interpretative circle. As described above, in IPA analysis is a cyclical process. In it, the researcher's role is to make sense of the person trying to make sense of their experience. To help visualise this some of its proponents have used images of circles, one denoting the person and another denoting the researcher. The two circles touch at one point. This 'coming together' changes as the researcher adopts the phenomenological attitude through bracketing of knowledge, however gained, and interprets data through rethinking and seeing the data afresh. These processes and the outcome of them impact on the movement around the circle and the extent of the touching. Constantly cyclical, the movement undertaken by the researcher helps to discover meaning within the data. Albeit the models if drawn are static, both afford the opportunity to show what IPA proponents call the enlivened cycle (Gil-Rodriguez and Hefferon 2012: 20; Vicary 2017: 69–70).

The meaning-making aspect of phenomenological research is itself complex and perhaps the least tangible element to grasp. Paley suggests little about the concept is really discussed in the literature, drawing attention to what meaning is and how it is distilled in the research processes (Paley 2017). Attention to the detail of this hermeneutic element is important throughout all aspects of the research design, methods and procedure which we will explore further in Part 2.

Idiography

For IPA, the final – yet as important – theoretical underpinning of the methodological approach is idiography, and this means two things: first, the focus on the person in a particular context, which is not a focus on the person per se but on the phenomenon and what it means for that person. As Smith et al. state, a reiteration of the complexity of the phenomenological concept of experience or on grasping the meaning of something for a given person cannot be conflated exactly with a focus on the individual (Smith et al. 2009: 29; Smith et al. 2022: 24). Second, IPA recommends detailed examination of a particular or single case. This examination, always undertaken in the first instance, sometimes remains as a case in its own right. However, there may also be a process which moves from examination of a single case to examination across cases and ultimately more general claims, now referred to in the newest edition by Smith et al. as personal experiential statements and general experiential statements (Smith et al. 2022: 86-87). While recommending caution, IPA additionally allows examination of similarities and differences across cases. This examination, it is suggested, produces fine-grained accounts of patterns of meaning for persons reflecting upon a shared experience (Smith et al. 2009: 38) and remains a priority; albeit in time larger corpuses of cases may lead to the ability to consider the more general features of a particular phenomenon (Vicary 2017: 72; Smith et al. 2022: 31–32).

The assumption so far is that experience, and especially the lived experience, are commonly understood concepts. However, this understanding is not as straightforward as might first appear. In this chapter we will now discuss experience as it is understood in relation to IPA.

Experience

Levels

The explanation of experience as provided by IPA proponents is based on Dilthey (1976) in Smith et al. (2009: 2; Smith et al. 2022: 2). Described is a hierarchy or different levels, the first or elemental level is one in which a person is absorbed constantly and unconsciously on the everyday flow of experience. The second, higher level is where the person begins to become conscious of what is happening or has an experience. This stage reaches its height, or comprehensive level, where the experience has a larger significance and comprises aspects of a person's life. It is these aspects which are the focus of research studies using IPA as its methodological approach. In Smith et al. (2009), the example given is that of a person undergoing major surgery in which the parts, such as receiving the diagnosis, preparing for surgery, recovery and so on, although separated by time, are linked by common meaning. IPA seeks to engage with the person making sense of the comprehensive experience and especially with the meaning the person is making of it. The part the researcher plays is to enable the person to recount the comprehensive experience by asking them to describe and reflect upon it (Vicary 2017: 74–75).

In addition, and of noteworthy resonance with social work, IPA uses the concept of lived experience. Again, borrowing from phenomenology and in particular Husserl (Finlay 2008), understanding what is meant by the concept of lived experience is fundamental to any phenomenological research, a term often used but perhaps also misrepresented or oversimplified.

Lived experience and layers of the lifeworld

We are seeking in IPA research to enter the lifeworld of a person, to understand what it is like to experience the phenomena of interest. Vagle reminds us of the phenomenological tradition of concern with the 'essence' of human lived experience (Vagle 2018). By trying to get to the structure and texture of the experience through IPA, the detailed nature of the experience can be uncovered. The lifeworld is therefore multi-dimensional, characterised by van Manen (2014) as universal themes or lifeworld existentials. Temporality, spatiality, corporeality, relationality and materiality are integrated, fundamental aspects of a person's lifeworld (van Manen 2014). In rudimentary terms these aspects span how a phenomenon is experienced in relation to felt, subjective time, space, the body, relations with others, and material things. This helps us to conceptualise the lifeworld and lived experience as a human and embodied entity; these are ideas that we will return to in Chapter 5. The distinction made between a passing experience is one that is asserted or what IPA views as lived and, because it is lived, can be reflected upon. As we have intimated, reflection is key to understanding experience and to the practice of IPA research. In relation to layers, IPA encapsulates lived experience in the description of their sequence, each signifying an increased degree of reflection (Smith et al. 2009: 189; Smith et al. 2022: 136–39). In turn, the first layer of experience has as its foundation the immediate flow, minimal level or pre-reflective reflection based on Sartre. The second involves intuitive, undirected reflection including daydreams, imagination and memory. The next layer involves reflection that is attentive, occurring when an experience has significance, is recognised as such and warrants consideration. In IPA, the conscious unpeeling of each layer is central and leads to the next layer of controlled reflection in which there is formal assessment and reflection upon events. Smith and colleagues refer to these layers as the individual's bandwidth in which they are engaged in reflection themselves (Smith et al. 2009: 190; Smith et al. 2022: 136). It is into this reflective loop that the researcher enters and does so to enable the person to give an account of their reflections upon the major experience or phenomenon. Giving voice to the participants is identified as the fundamental goal of phenomenological research (Larkin et al. 2006). In what could be recognised as a fourth layer, the researcher will therefore ignite new reflections both unconscious (layer two and three) and deliberate (layer four) which in research terms are the findings that arise in the analysis thereof (Smith et al. 2009: 190; Vicary 2017: 75; Smith et al. 2022: 137).

Conclusion

In this chapter we have outlined the inception and development of IPA, a relatively recent methodological approach which is underpinned by a trio of borrowed theoretical influences. Applied using research terminology, we have situated this methodological approach in an interpretative qualitative tradition which seeks to uncover meaning of a particular phenomenon as it is experienced by a person. The emphasis on experience, its structure and texture are of central importance to this approach along with the sense-making, both by the person and in turn the researcher. As noted, the role of the latter is crucial. Identity and emotional experience are the main constructs to have emerged in IPA studies to date and are also the focus of much social work research IPA, itself a result of an intellectual debate in health psychology about which paradigm best suits which research agenda (Smith 1996, 2004). Meanwhile, adopting the phenomenological attitude, or bracketing, is also of central importance given the professional experience of the researcher and the need to put to one side pre-existing understanding of the personal professional background of the researcher and of the impact of professional background.

Summary points

- **Three components:** IPA is underpinned by three theories – idiography, phenomenology and hermeneutics.
- **Giving voice:** IPA seeks to understand, give voice and make meaning of a phenomenon or person in context parallel with social work.
- **Meaning:** Both IPA and social work attempt to uncover the nature and meaning of the reality of people's experiences.
- **Interpretative process:** The role of the interpreter is key.

IPA is particularly suited to the professional skill base of the social work researcher and more readily enables the double hermeneutic as it is understood, in the two ways outlined in this chapter. It is this 'fit' for social work which we will now go on to discuss in Chapter 2.

2 The purpose of research in social work

Chapter aims:

- to consider the purpose of research for social work practice
- to explore the fit between social work, social work research and IPA
- to briefly discuss other methodological approaches which might be considered
- to critique IPA and its possible limitations as a methodological approach for social work research.

Introduction

In this chapter we consider the purpose of research in social work, including a discussion about the similarities and differences between social work practice and social work research. First, we discuss the developments in social work research, particularly the rise in evidence-based social work and the debate which this has given rise to in relation to which research methodological approaches for social work research are best suited. We will then consider the 'fit' between social work and qualitative social work research based on a dialogue that started in the United States before considering social work, social work research and IPA. To do so, we undertake a brief discussion of other methodologies (although not exhaustive) usually associated with social work research and which could also be considered a good 'fit', namely, Grounded Theory, Ethnomethodology, Narrative and Action Research. Last, we take the opportunity to focus on the interface between social work research and the use of IPA.

Developments in research for social work

Of suggested ways in which IPA could expand, one is its use by associated professional research disciplines such as medicine (Smith 2011a). Although this proposed development is advocated by other commentators, there is also a concern as to how readily researchers from positivist research traditions will accept the validity of IPA as a methodology (Shaw 2011). Certainly, this present book is arguing for its use other than in psychology and where the subject area is a different discipline, that of social work and research for social work.

The purpose of research for social work has attracted commentary in which it is increasingly argued that much in the same manner as health, social work requires an evidence base. A helpful summary has been discussed by Webb (2001) in which he includes a potted chronology of these developments in the UK from Townsend's call for research evidence in the 1970s through to commentators such as MacDonald and Sheldon in the 1990s (Sheldon 2001). Webb suggests that there are five threads to this chronology and a common theme: the idea that practice based on scientific evidence can produce a social service that is effective and more accountable (Webb 2001: 59). Webb questions the validity of this theme. Instead, he suggests that a reliance on evidence achieved through scientific methods such as experiments might undermine professional judgement and discretion, thereby restricting practice (Webb 2001: 57). He later suggests that such evidence alone is difficult to translate into the social work context in which decisions are 'contaminated by complexities' (Webb 2002: 49) and extends this notion of complexity and the challenge it gives if using such 'hard' evidence in social work. He refers, for example, to the findings of a study of social work practitioner views on research in which it is reported that participants acknowledged evidence and its complexity but are also mindful of the impact of knowing and feeling in practice (Shaw and Shaw in Webb 2002: 50). In a more recent discussion, others question whether social work research is particular to the field (Shaw 2018: 17). Shaw concludes that research into social work should be rigorous both in theory and concept and when it is based on empirical pursuit must have a sound strategy and methodology (Shaw 2018). In short, significant inquiry into social work or social work research which aims to underpin social work practice should, as with all applied research, be relevant to and for its practice. It is in this context that we now look in more detail at the relationship between social work and qualitative social work research.

Social work and qualitative social work research

A long-standing discussion about the 'fit' between social work as a practice and social work as a research mode or qualitative social work research, probably first began in the United States in a debate between two authors of social work research methodology: Jane Gilgun and Deborah Padgett. Mindful that their language use differs slightly to that which is normally deployed in the United Kingdom, the discussion, encapsulated in several publications, (Gilgun 1994; Padgett 1998a; Padgett 1998b) nonetheless gives a good insight and is summarised here: purpose, relationship between the worker and the person and reason. Gilgun (1994: 123–24) is of the opinion that qualitative social work research is a good fit for social work or, as she terms it, hand within glove. For Gilgun, the focus on the perspective of the person is congruent with the underlying philosophy in social work which is to start where the person is.

Moreover, that the person is inextricably linked and is part of the wider context is also the same. Neither argument is disputed by Padgett. As such, and as this book argues, IPA also can be considered a good fit. We return to this in more detail in Chapter 3.

There is, however, some divergence. Gilgun suggests that the detailed description of individual cases fit with the social work injunction to individualise assessment, treatment and evaluation to fit specific situations. Padgett contends that the researcher's ultimate responsibility lies in contributing knowledge and understanding in the form of rigorous scholarship, not in providing a service. While specifically referring to Grounded Theory as a methodological approach, Gilgun goes on to suggest that the combination of induction and deduction parallels how a social worker thinks about cases using previous research, theory and practice wisdom while attempting to avoid imposing preconceptions. For Gilgun, ultimately, both the researcher and the social worker come to conclusions about situations, after interacting with them and after gathering as much data as possible, albeit these are tentative and open to modification as new information becomes available. From the perspective of IPA as a research methodology in social work, the aim is to contribute knowledge about the lived experience of people who are using or receiving social work services and in turn to underpin best practice for the social workers who deliver these. IPA is, however, an interpretivist approach which seeks to make sense of a particular lived experience at a particular time. Findings may therefore be applicable in that circumstance and may not apply to the whole. However, IPA's strength is the in-depth knowledge that it brings.

Regarding methods of data collection and record keeping, both Gilgun and Padgett agree that data collection methods such as interviewing, observation and document analysis are used by social workers as well as by qualitative social work researchers (Grounded Theorists). In addition, the use of field notes, observer comments and memos parallel process recording and problem-oriented case record keeping. Padgett also adds that qualitative interviewing in particular bears a strong resemblance to a therapeutic interview. After Weiss, Padgett suggests that the parallels are many: both types of interviewing allow thoughts, memories and feelings to be disclosed in a 'safe' non-judgemental environment established by an empathic interviewer (Weiss 1994 in Padgett 1998b) and that both entail a joint search for meaning and understanding. The vocabulary deployed by Padgett, including meaning making, resonates well with IPA as we have seen in Chapter 1; we continue to explore IPA and its fit for social work in Chapter 3 and Part 2.

A further consideration in the Gilgun/Padgett debate is context. Gilgun points out that both social work and social work research often take place in natural settings; for social workers, this can mean in the homes and communities of the person in much the same way as a researcher would engage with their participants. It is increasingly the case that data collection for research is taking place through online media, and that electronic-based interventions are developing in social work practice, driven most recently by an unprecedented global pandemic and increased availability of technology; but neither is yet normative. We will explore the mechanics of data collection in more detail in Part 2.

In addition, and perhaps most obviously, both Gilgun and Padgett agree that social work practice involves direct engagement with people through which they strive for empathy, and that this is characterised by a balance between being in tune with clients and maintaining an analytical stance. Padgett, however, warns caution. She points out that the ethical and legal ramifications of social (clinical) work, particularly mandated reporting, require special attention when conducting qualitative research. She suggests that the dilemma that arises from the ethical obligation that all qualitative researchers have must ensure the confidentiality of data. Registered [licensed] social workers [clinicians] who are also researchers cannot give an absolute guarantee of confidentiality because they must abide by mandated reporting laws. Researcher-social workers [clinicians] conducting studies in which abuse may be revealed should tell participants in advance that the need to maintain confidentiality may be overridden because of this legal requirement. Including such a caveat in the informed consent form allows potential respondents to be fully appraised of the consequences of participation. Such moral and ethical considerations for IPA and social work are discussed further in Part 2.

A final, possible difference between social workers and social work researchers as suggested by Padgett is that of education and training; social work education she suggests draws on the unique configuration of coursework in practice and a curriculum that explores human behaviour, social welfare and research. Of essential importance are placement (supervised internships) in agencies where students are given hands-on experience in direct practice. For Padgett, the exposure for these students to social science theories and methods are necessarily reduced by the need to train future practitioners.

When considering IPA as a research methodology in social work using the Gilgun/Padgett debate as a framework IPA undoubtedly also has many synergies with social work. We now undertake a brief examination of IPA and other popular methodological approaches starting with Grounded Theory.

Social work research, IPA and other methodological approaches

As suggested above, and as will be explored in more detail in Part 2, IPA is particularly suited to the professional skill base of social workers; in the tradition of the double hermeneutic, social workers interview in an open manner and critically analyse information. However, as has been debated earlier in this chapter, while the skills used are similar the purpose of a social work interview and an interview conducted for research differs. We will now briefly consider other methodological approaches beginning with Grounded Theory, including Constructivist Grounded Theory, Ethnomethodology, Narrative and last Action Research, albeit this is not an exhaustive list. Indeed, Smith and colleagues also discuss Discourse Analysis (Smith et al. 2022: 38–41). Further exploration of Grounded Theory, Constructivist Grounded Theory and Ethnomethodology can be found in Sarah's thesis (Vicary 2017: 81–85). The location is given here for ease.

Grounded Theory and Constructivist Grounded Theory

In much the same way as IPA has developed as a counter to the more positivist approaches to research in the field of health psychology research, Grounded Theory was developed in the 1960s by two sociologists as a response to the then-dominant tradition of positivist or quantitative approaches (Glaser and Strauss 1967). Hitherto, there is little doubt that qualitative research was viewed as invalid because of the perception that it lacked robust, replicable techniques and in turn rigour and validity. Since the publication of the seminal text describing Grounded Theory as a methodology and its techniques by Glaser and Strauss in 1967 several versions have emerged, primarily because of a dispute about its nature (Glaser and Strauss 1967). This debate focused, ironically, on rigour and is taken up by others less comfortable with Grounded Theory's positivist elements (Strauss and Corbin 1990). One significant version is that developed by Charmaz (2008) who positions what she termed Constructivist Grounded Theory as a middle ground between this quantitative and qualitative debate (Puddephatt 2006: 9; Vicary 2017: 80–81).

Grounded theory, and in particular Constructivist Grounded Theory, is not unusual as a potential alternative methodology for studies also considering IPA (Smith et al. 2009: 201; Smith et al. 2022: 38). However, there are differences which pertain, not least some argue that there is room for creativity and freedom within IPA (Willig 2001: 69). In addition, Grounded Theory focuses, just as IPA does, on the individual. However, for Grounded Theory the focus is on how the individual constructs and make sense of the world, or their reality, and in turn a theory emerges as constructed by the researcher. For IPA, the researcher enables the individual to make sense of the phenomenon and in turn makes sense of this meaning-making (Vicary 2017: 81).

There are also pragmatic considerations for using IPA instead of Grounded Theory when the suggested sample type and size is taken into account. While both methodologies initially use purposive sampling to recruit participants who have experienced the phenomenon being studied, Grounded Theory also uses theoretical sampling. The researcher adds further individuals to the sample to explore the found theory until theoretical saturation is reached. Although this does not happen at an exact point, sample sizes tend therefore to be large. IPA focuses on the individual in a particular context, and a detailed account of their experience is said to be sufficient. In essence, there is no 'need' to go beyond the individual (Vicary 2017: 86).

Moreover, the general rule of thumb espoused by those who use Grounded Theory is that data collection and the analysis of the generated data takes place concurrently (Glaser 1992; Glaser and Strauss 1967 in Charmaz 2008: 83). Corresponding collection and analysis involve the researcher in undertaking the process of data collection and analysis as coterminous processes. The one, in essence, drives the other, and vice versa, and the process moves through induction to deduction. Simultaneous involvement in data collection and analysis is said to mean that the emerging analysis shapes data collection decisions (Charmaz 2008: 85). Researchers deploy Grounded Theory to generate theory from the data which is then constantly compared with further data instances.

Theory is said to be discovered by examining concepts grounded in the data (Starks and Trinidad 2007: 1373). Theories generated are open to generalisation and refutability. In research which seeks to understand social work from the perspective of those with lived experience of receipt of social work services, it may not be practical or indeed ethical for the researcher to engage in such a reiterative data collection and analysis process; repeated iterations to test emerging theory may be intrusive and may involve potential for breach of confidentiality (Vicary 2017: 83).

Ethnomethodology

The term Ethnomethodology was devised in the early 1950s and published in a series of papers brought together in a single book by Garfinkel in 1967. Here the author describes ethnomethodological studies as a focus on 'the objective reality of social facts as an ongoing accomplishment of the concerted activities of daily life, with the ordinary, artful ways of that accomplishment being by members known, used, and taken for granted' (Garfinkel 1967: vii). Ethnomethodology is a discursive methodology described in three parts (Vicary 2017: 84):

- ethno – which refers to members of a social scene
- methods – which refers to the things that members routinely do to create and recreate the various mutually recognisable social actions or social practices
- ology – which means the study of these methods (Rawls 2002: 6).

Briefly, ethnomethodology is the study of the methods that members (of society) use to produce recognisable social interaction. The research questions which mostly fit this methodology are about 'doing being' and as such are suited to inquiry into social work. However, there is an important difference. In social work the researcher is exploring experience for the person and interpreting it. There are other subtle differences. For example, in ethnomethodology, the focus is shared interaction and not the individual per se. Thus, the part the researcher plays in ethnomethodology means the interaction remains in the transcript and subject to analysis. In IPA, the experience of the individual – their inner thoughts feelings and emotions and how they make sense of experience – is foremost. The part the researcher plays is to prompt the telling of the experience and to encourage awareness of the comprehensive level. The central role of the researcher thereafter is to interpret the telling in depth. This interpretation is the double hermeneutic: the researcher showing empathy and then questioning in trying to make sense of the participant trying to make sense of their experience (Vicary 2017: 84).

Like IPA, Ethnomethodology also views the participants as actively making meaning in the interview situation with the interaction involving work to construct a mutually intelligible world. However, in IPA the interviewer prompts but does not share. Their role is to allow the participant to explore the sense they are making of their experience to provide a rich, detailed, first-person account (Smith et al. 2009: 56; Smith et al. 2022: 53). Ethnomethodology is concerned with language in use and that it is through shared, mutually agreed use that meaning is created. Language both builds understanding of reality and defines the way in which individuals enact identity. IPA, rather, relies on language but through the interpretation of the researcher, even to the extent that the researcher may 'see things' in the data that the participant does not, as is the interpretative basis of IPA. This might also pose a dilemma (Vicary 2017: 85).

Narrative

Narrative approaches are popular in the human sciences for tuning into the story of a person's life. Kohler Riessman, however, cautions against regarding this as a simplistic endeavour and highlights different analytic methods for gathering, analysing and interpreting Narrative data (Riessman 2008). For social work, Narrative is important as people communicate through the stories of what is happening to them and their families. Narrative also helps people convey what has happened in the past and can serve different functions for both the storyteller and the listener (Riessman 2008). Narrative analysis is most often rooted in study of the particular so appeals to the idiographic interest in social work. There are also multiple ways that people can share their stories creatively using verbal and non-verbal techniques. The concept of truth emerges in any discussion about use of stories whether research or otherwise; the term itself often suggests a fictional account (Riessman 2008). Subjective reality has been considered in Chapter 1 as a central element of phenomenological research, but discussions about truth remain controversial in social work practice and decision-making. Careful design of Narrative research will consider the nature and function of the story in the meaning-making process. Narrative data can powerfully highlight lived reality and is often threaded with linguistic signs that illuminate important aspects while selecting what remains less visible.

Action Research

Action Research is a shorthand term given to the type of exploration that involves practitioners researching their own practice and working environment to contribute to the development of the profession. As a practitioner-based approach, it appears well suited to the practice of social work – especially as it is conducted in the workplace. It concerns a cycle of planning, acting, observing and reflecting (Susman and Evered 1978; Kemmis 2010; McAteer 2013). Drawing from the work of Shaw and Lunt (2018), Action Research in social work includes a focus on the researcher's own practice and that of close peers in which the researcher is directly involved in setting outcomes and objectives designed to be of practical benefit to professionals, service providers and people who are in receipt of services. Types of Action Research have evolved, including participatory action research which in turn engages those who are being researched as co researchers.

Critiques of this approach to research tend to revolve around the positionality of the researcher as an insider and in turn the possible impact this might have in being too close to any data resulting in subjectivity. Moreover, it is suggested that the researcher may be unable to stand away from any assumptions, a process mitigated against in IPA through bracketing. Last, it is claimed that this type of research can focus more on the action than the research (Fongkaew and Nilvarangkul 2018).

As discussed in Chapter 1, the epistemological basis is particularly pertinent when considering the use of IPA as the methodology for social work since such research primarily wishes to understand and explore an experience within its social and cultural context, albeit its psychological depth has been critiqued because of its lack of other considerations not least a sociological breadth (Houston and Mullan-Jensen, 2011), a debate to which we return when we consider the future direction of social work and IPA in Chapter 8.

Conclusion

In this chapter we have explored the synergy between social work and social work research and discussed the similarities and differences between them. We have briefly explored developments in social work research particularly that of evidence-based social work and discussed the 'fit' between social work and qualitative social work research, based on a dialogue that started in the United States. In relation to which methodological approaches for social work research are a best fit, we then considered other methodologies usually associated with social work research, Grounded Theory (including Constructivist Grounded Theory), Ethnomethodology, Narrative and Action Research.

In so doing, we argue that research using IPA that explores the lived experience of a person in receipt of social work services is less intrusive and has fewer ethical challenges for the participant. We propose that the role of the researcher, the dynamics of the research and the ontological positioning are fundamental and perhaps more readily fit with IPA. As such it is a good methodological fit since it explores experience and specifically the sense made of it from the viewpoint of an individual or homogenous group. Furthermore, IPA affords the exploration of convergence and divergence, if any, between the understanding and experience of participants from within the same group. Pragmatically, it may not be possible, as is the expectation for example in Grounded Theory, to keep returning to points of data collection until theory has been saturated. IPA is increasingly being conducted in other subject areas including the health and other allied professional arenas and, as this book is considering, in social work. But IPA's use in social work has its critics; social work research may also seek to explore the psychological experience of participants whilst positioned in the surrounding sociological and political context. One of the limitations of IPA is that it may have psychological depth but lacks the breadth of social context, a critique to which we return in Chapter 8.

Summary points

- **Diversity:** There are important differences in methodological approaches.
- **Details matter:** Understanding the nuances of IPA can help you consider methods.
- **Fit for social work:** IPA has an excellent fit for social work research.
- **Three components:** Idiography, phenomenology and hermeneutics combine in IPA.

We have explored different approaches to research and now turn to consider more of the details involved in setting up an effective IPA social work research study. Chapter 3 introduces a holistic model which draws together the key ingredients of IPA social work research.

3 | Introducing an integrated holistic model for IPA social work research

Chapter aims:

- to introduce an integrated holistic model for social work IPA
- to explore your roles, interests and perspectives
- to consider the ethical foundations and research focus
- to propose the importance of an effective support network to guide you
- to confirm your rationale and justification for using IPA.

Introduction

Chapters 1 and 2 have provided a discussion about social work, social work research and IPA. This chapter now considers how to prepare for embarking on a social work IPA research journey that sustains commitment to this methodology at each stage. Every aspect of the research design is a crucial element, to generate rich phenomenological description that will lead to enhanced understanding through your sense-making quest. The research design must demonstrate commitment to the integrated components of IPA as outlined in our earlier chapters. Chapter 3 shifts the focus from understanding IPA as an approach for social work research, to a discussion about the practicalities.

Attention to the research design sets the necessary foundation for authentic encounters with people where their experiences are powerfully revealed, valued and interpreted. The researcher can build on this foundation to maintain discipline and self-awareness as their study develops. This chapter introduces an integrated, holistic model for IPA social work research that weaves the essential ingredients together. We will then explore each component, discuss how these come together in an effective study and establish key points about social work research and practice. Extracts from a dialogue between the authors and examples from their respective research will be used throughout to illustrate different IPA social work research projects.

An integrated, holistic process of IPA for social work

It is almost a truism to assert that the choice of topic for research goes hand in hand with choice of methodology. Vagle (2018) proposes that phenomenological research is an immersive and embodied process that is crafted to gain deeper understanding of everyday experiences. The researcher constructs the study and connects many elements as part of this dynamic crafting process. Embarking on the journey of an IPA study therefore involves creating a holistic design that weaves essential elements together. The integrated elements which form the whole of an effective IPA social work study are shown in the model in Figure 3.1. This model is introduced to explore and guide how to practically craft your IPA research.

The elements in Figure 3.1 are dynamic as part of the ongoing research process; however, the research design is rooted in firm, ethical foundations. Building on these foundations your study design needs to incorporate methods and procedures that will provide the phenomenological, hermeneutic and idiographic aspects of IPA. These methods and procedures need to elicit data that can be explored in the sense-making cycles to reveal interpreted accounts of lived experience. Woven throughout the holistic model is the researcher's reflexive process and the support that will guide them through. We will return to support through supervision in Chapter 7.

This chapter will explore effective design of IPA research, highlighting the importance of the foundations and focus, before considering choice of methods. The integrated elements of the model will be considered. Although we will explore the different elements in sequence, it is important to remember these form part of the whole of your crafted research study shown in Figure 3.1.

Figure 3.1 Holistic model of IPA for social work research and practice

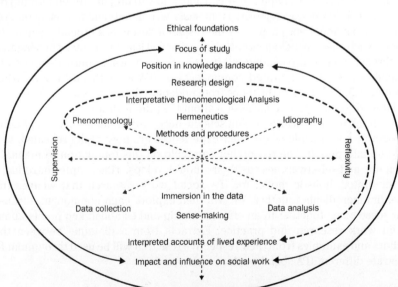

Different ways to design your IPA social work study

Once you have selected IPA, you will develop a design for your research that is suited to your interests and the phenomenon under investigation. We use two research examples in this book to explore aspects of IPA for social work and introduce these here. Both these example studies come from the authors' doctoral research studies which used IPA. They are not included to provide a blueprint for research or to suggest that these are of a better quality than any other studies. We are using these simply to explore the nuances of the research process as experienced by the authors to demonstrate how the integrated components of IPA come together in social work research. You can see how the different studies were crafted in line with the respective researcher's interests and skills and within the context of social work phenomena. You might be exploring a very different focus, or the lived experiences of those who are recipients of social work services. You might be exploring a specific aspect of lived experience to develop more understanding of particular issues that are facing individuals or families. We hope to promote reflection and prompt you to make the right design choices for your own focus and scale of study.

Example Study 1—An Interpretative Phenomenological Analysis of the impact of professional background on role fulfilment: a study of approved mental health practice (Vicary 2017)

Sarah's doctoral research study explored the impact of professional background on the experience of approved mental health professionals (AMHPs) and their role undertaking assessments under the Mental Health Act 1983 in England and Wales. This research aimed to find out whether professional background had any impact on the fulfilment of this role, and the detail of how this was experienced by the participants in her study. Statutory functions of the AMHP role previously carried out by social work were extended to other mental health professionals. A crucial aspect of the study was the sociological and political context with the focus on a specific role undertaken by social workers, and other professionals, within the context of mental health practice in England. Sarah's own professional experience as a qualified social worker and experienced AMHP was central to the motivation for her study.

Example Study 2—'When David Bowie Created Ziggy Stardust': the lived experiences of social workers' learning in the workplace (Ferguson 2021)

Gillian's doctoral research study explored the lived experiences of social workers learning through their daily work. The study was focused on the intersection of knowledge about workplace and professional learning and explored social workers' unique lived experiences. The title was drawn from a striking metaphor used by a social worker to describe his experience of learning, in which he created a new persona to navigate the landscape and tasks of practice. This specific study was undertaken in Scotland and positioned in the context of social work education and continuing professional learning in that nation.

A crucial lens of this research study was the use of workplace learning theory alongside understanding the strategic and local context of learning. Gillian's primary motivation for the study stemmed from her role in workforce learning and development in local authority settings.

The chapter will explore the authors' roles and perspectives that were influential in the focus and design of these example studies as part of the discussion. We will also explore how the example studies fit with the elements of the integrated model and sustained commitment to IPA.

Choosing and justifying IPA

We have discussed IPA as a choice of methodology in Chapters 1 and 2. You might have already decided that IPA is right for your study, or this may still be under consideration. It is important that you select an approach that is right for the focus of your research and develop a clear rationale for your choice. Choosing IPA was a pivotal moment for both authors, part of a process in which they had each considered many other options. Both Sarah and Gillian describe a sense of fit with IPA when they encountered this research approach. Sarah said:

> I really engaged with the underpinning theory and the phenomenological, philosophical basis. For me, philosophy is about understanding where you are in the world. Getting the right methodological approach was a hugely important step for me. It was more than just finding out about something, or what something was like for a person, but that connection to the importance of meaning. I had to work out what research I could do that was pragmatic, realistic in the time I had available to me. The philosophical and the hermeneutic both appealed to me. So did you choose IPA, or did it choose you?

Gillian said:

> I started looking at phenomenology and got very excited about it, but I was at risk of getting too stuck into the philosophy without having a practical angle to my study. That's why I chose IPA over a more purist possible phenomenological approach. There was an appeal in the three components of IPA, so it sounds like we both made a pragmatic decision triggered by an interest in the philosophy.

Both were attracted by the philosophical basis but felt that there was a risk that they could become too immersed in this if they chose a more purist phenomenological approach. Personal and professional motivation were strongly evident in choice of IPA, and both were determined to have a practical outcome for their respective research projects. Gillian:

> I thought it would be slightly more practical to manage. So, I suppose that is very similar to what you're saying about the pragmatic decision because I did feel that I was going to go down the philosophical rabbit hole. I think important, the distinction between phenomenology as research and phenomenology

as philosophy. You do have to understand enough about each but remember that it is research that you are going to be doing.

Sarah:

> I could never square the idea of quantitative research in my head, it didn't make sense to me at all, particularly in relation to social work studies and my social work practice. I always saw people as individuals as opposed to groups of people using the services. I started making connections between me as a social work practitioner and me as a social work researcher.

Sarah highlights her developing researcher identity with connections to her social work practitioner identity. One of the important aspects of IPA is the alignment of her interest in how people make sense of their experiences in her practice and therefore within the research process. A desire to understand social work issues is strongly linked with making practical changes too. Gillian:

> I wanted to be doing something that was very practical within the workplace. I wanted to improve workplace learning opportunities for social workers, but I was needing to explore lived experiences to get to the heart of understanding what was even meant by learning in that context. I came to this point when I was doing the literature review and thought, we don't even know what we're talking about, so it is premature to think about improving it?

Both researchers were able to see how IPA provided an approach that resonated with social work practice, and which drew on skills and knowledge to help explore and make sense of experience. Sarah:

> IPA will always appeal to those who are interested in what it is like to be in the human condition. But I think that has got huge connection to social work, because if you are interested in people and you're interested in how their world is, it's not just understanding the lifeworld but trying to understand how people make sense of their existence. The hermeneutic side of it.

Gillian:

> Yes, if you think of some practice frameworks in social work, you know sometimes we refer to 'my world' concepts, we are trying to get a sense of the person's world. It's about trying to get to that essence of, for example, what is it like to be a child living in these conditions, with these issues happening in the family and what is that like as part of your social work assessment, so I think there is a big connection there too.

The origins and focus of your research study are important. We have considered the different roles and perspectives that might have influenced your social work study. Your initial ideas might also be influenced by the scale of the study you plan to do: for example, whether this is a small practitioner piece of research, a doctoral project or a larger scale project. You will likely have a clear idea about the overall topic of research that you want to carry out. You might have a specific area of practice or issue that you are passionate about exploring or improving. The final research focus and questions which the authors sought to explore were the result of a process of refining from initial ideas. If you have chosen IPA, then your focus can be refined clearly to explore the experiences of people who can provide insight into your topic and the meaning of this for them. For IPA it is essential to refine your focus so that the research design can help you gather the kind of data which will provide insight stemming from the unique experiences of people. Think about the overall topic that you are planning to study. How can you refine your focus? Getting your focus clear might take a few attempts, and for most researchers this is a changing and integral part of the process in the initial stages. Sustaining commitment to the IPA process is easier when your focus is clear.

We have highlighted some of the influential factors that led the authors to choose IPA for the two example studies that were introduced. As discussed in Chapter 2, there were many other research approaches that could have been used by Sarah and Gillian; however, the focus and subsequent findings would be very different. Table 3.1 shows how different methodology choices would have altered the focus of the example studies and their respective research questions.

Table 3.1 A comparison of methodologies

Methodology: Disciplinary origin and principles	What this would mean for the focus and research questions in the example studies
Grounded Theory Interpretivist Sociology Uncovering social processes, influences and impacts	**Example 1:** Development of theory about how professionals fulfill the AMHP role Research Question: What factors influence how professionals fulfill the AMHP role? **Example 2:** Development of theory about how social workers Learn in the workplace Research Question: What factors influence how social workers learn in the workplace?
Action Research Interpretivist Democratic participation Involving participants in creation of knowledge	**Example 1:** Testing ways of fulfilling the AMHP role from different professional backgrounds Research Question: What are the ways that AMHPs fulfill their role? **Example 2:** Testing ways of improving workplace learning for social workers Research Question: What are the ideas social workers have about improving learning in the workplace?

(continued)

Table 3.1 (*Continued*)

Methodology: Disciplinary origin and principles	What this would mean for the focus and research questions in the example studies
Ethnography/ Autoethnography/ Ethnomethodology Interpretivist Anthropology Learning cultural patterns through observing people in their natural environment	**Example 1:** Observation of approved mental health professionals fulfilling their statutory role Research Question: How do approved mental health professionals from different backgrounds fulfill their role? **Example 2:** Observation of what happens in the workplace and where learning occurs for social workers Research Question: How do social workers learn in their workplace?
Narrative Interpretivist Human storytelling and education Capturing stories Sense-making	**Example 1:** Stories and case studies of approved mental health professionals from their practice Research Question: What are the stories approved mental health professionals tell about their fulfilling their role? **Example 2:** Stories and case studies of the learning experiences and journeys of social workers Research question: What are the stories social workers tell about their learning in the workplace?
Phenomenology/ Hermeneutics Interpretivist Philosophy Understanding individual experience and examining how individuals make sense of experience	**Example 1:** Depth and focus on the essence of the lived experience of approved mental health professionals. Insights into the sense approved mental health professionals make of their unique lived experience Research Question: What are the lived experiences of approved mental health professionals fulfilling their role? **Example 2:** Depth and focus on the essence of the lived experience of social workers learning in the workplace. Insights into the sense social workers make of their unique lived experience Research Question: What are the experiences of social workers learning in the workplace?

In summary, IPA draws from a range of phenomenological approaches to research and the specific focus is on 'personal meaning, sense-making in a particular context for people who share a particular experience' (Smith et al. 2009: 45). Deciding on IPA as an approach is an important step in shaping your study. Think about where you are in the process of choosing your methodology. You might still be ambivalent about the best approach or have already decided that IPA is the best fit. Keep thinking about the intention of your study. Our holistic model of IPA for social work research positions ethical foundations and the focus of your study as an essential component. We will now consider how to build these ethical foundations and establish a meaningful focus for your study.

Position of your study in the knowledge landscape

Positioning your study in the wider context is important at different stages in your research. The literature search and review is one of the contextual elements of any research study. The position of the literature review in IPA and phenomenological research more broadly is much debated. Vagle (2018) suggests an extensive literature review can interfere with openness to exploring phenomenon. Dahlberg et al. similarly suggest that 'knowing too much can make it hard to bridle' in phenomenological research (Dahlberg et al. 2008: 174). You are likely to be coming to your research with a strong interest in the phenomenon you want to explore or have specific existing expertise in. Practice knowledge and wisdom might not only inform what you have decided to study, but also how your ultimate findings will be used. We would argue that positioning your proposed study in the knowledge landscape is an important element of an IPA study at the outset and at the findings stage when you have generated new insights. At the outset it is therefore important to have a clear plan for a literature review strategy that will enable you to position your study in relation to existing knowledge and indeed where there are perceived gaps in this. Think about what is informing the shape of your study and where your research fits in the knowledge landscape. In the authors' example studies, the research questions arose directly from the practice and policy context. In what ways does your existing knowledge inform your study? Where will any new knowledge that you generate fit? Think about the importance of bracketing your existing knowledge and the strategies for managing this as you continue your IPA journey; we will return to explore this in Chapter 5.

Embarking on your IPA journey

Embarking on your IPA research journey will most likely have a strong connection to your personal and professional interests. Your roles and perspectives are inextricably linked to the knowledge, intention and motivation that you bring to your social work research. You may come to your research with very different roles, previous experience or interest in a topic. Think about what your different roles might mean for your research and how these might assist or interfere with your study. You might be in a practitioner or operational role, a social work academic or a leadership role for the profession. You can see from the introduction to this book that the authors come to research with multiple roles and interests. Both researchers are qualified social workers and academics with some shared interests; however, their professional experience and personal backgrounds are very different. At the time of the example studies, the authors were in very different roles that influenced their research from the focus to the dissemination of their findings.

If you are an insider researcher (Ross 2017) it is essential to think about the pros and cons of your role. You may have easier access to participants or expertise that assists your research, however there may be conflicts of interest or risks associated with your findings. Your research site may be a specific social work service, in which case it may be difficult to ensure that this is not identifiable. Attention to the different types of information that could identify services or individuals will remain important. If you are a registered social worker or from a different background, think about how you will manage any tensions between your professional codes and your research ethics. Make clear any potential risks that participants should be aware of if they take part in the research. These are not always immediately apparent when participants come forward. How will you manage any situations where poor practice or potential harm is disclosed? What if conflicts of interest arise during the research?

It is helpful to think about what other people might expect from the research process and whether this aligns with your own vision or otherwise. It is also helpful to establish a firm foundation of the way that your research is connected to social work practice, or indeed, social work as an international movement. Gatekeepers will often have an important role in whether your research can take place, or in the dissemination of information about your study to potential participants. Think about who the gatekeepers might be and how they can help your study, and identify any ways that there may be a negative impact on your planned study. These are some of the initial issues to consider as you embark on your study. We will now explore more about the ethical foundations of an effective IPA social work study.

Building solid ethical foundations for your social work study

Social work is a profession rooted in ethical practice and research in this field is, not surprisingly, an ethical endeavour. Stutchbury and Fox (2009) provide an ethical appraisal framework for evaluating research design which covers 'consequential, ecological, relational and deontological' issues drawing together ideas from the work of Seedhouse and Flinders. These different ethical considerations can help you focus on how your study fits within the social work systems and broader context (ecological). Your expertise from different roles might help you understand the context. An effective moral approach to social work practice is mirrored in the research process where all aspects should consider potential harm, fairness and avoidance of wrongdoing (deontological). Professional codes of practice for social work across nations highlight the importance of ethics, fairness, reliability, promoting trust and autonomy. Promoting respect, upholding confidentiality and human rights are also at the heart of social work practice. Additionally, you should consider who will ultimately benefit from your study (consequential), what the possible outcomes might be and potential harm or unintended consequences. Will this be a particular group of people, individual families or professionals with specific roles? Social work research and practice are in essence sensitive and always deal with important aspects of people's lives (relational). Public attitudes to social work and social workers and the nature of practice issues might mean that there is extra sensitivity in research findings and provision of any open data as part of research projects. Ethical foundations are at the root of your initial design; however, they remain a dynamic component of how you undertake your study at all stages. Think about what some of the ethical issues might be for your study and how these can inform your research.

In the authors' example studies, ethics were foregrounded in the research design and formed a dynamic aspect of the research process. It was important to reflect on ethics at all stages.

Gillian:

> I thought a lot about potential ethical dilemmas because I was doing this study in a place that I worked. Some of the participants knew me and some did not, so I had to really plan and work through the pros and cons of that. I spent a lot of time on how people would be recruited in a way that was independent of me directly asking them. I also set up a lot of information for participants about how things would be managed, and in my mind I was thinking about continually negotiating consent as I would do in social work practice. It was not just something that was in the consent form.

Both Sarah and Gillian provided detailed information for participants in advance of the study which outlined how people could withdraw from the research, how confidentiality would be maintained and how any disclosures of misconduct would be managed. Ethical approval was sought from respective universities and through organisational gatekeepers including the National Health Service (NHS) and the Association of Directors of Adult Social Services (ADASS) in England and specific local authority Chief Social Work Officers (CSWO) in Scotland.

Gillian:

> At the outset I was looking for things that were a straightforward conflict of interest where maybe I'd worked too closely with someone. Some people might have perceived that I had a particular power because of specific roles in the organisation, so I had declared a lot of stuff in the participant information

sheet about this. Some of my roles changed during the data gathering stage of this study and I had a statutory role that I felt might compromise my relationship with some participants if there was any crossover with specific cases. Although there was not a conflict in the end, I was very worried about that sort of thing interfering and I think careful planning prevented things going all over the place.

The nature of IPA and methods for data collection were also outlined clearly for participants. Sarah used visual methods that were part of data collection, and these were explained in participant information. Confidentiality was crucial throughout the example studies, extending beyond the participant's name. Sarah:

I included information that each participant should not use identifiable names or places. This also included the rich picture that I asked for, that this should not depict the names of people or places. I made sure that information was clear about any issues that might come up which could be perceived as inappropriate conduct and how I would manage this. I also included how long the interview process would take; this was important given the pressures on practitioners' time.

Reflection on ethical issues was a key aspect integrated into the design and active process of the research studies.

Planning for reflexivity, supervision and support for your social work study

The holistic model for IPA social work research (see Figure 3.1) shows reflexivity and supervision as essential components that encircle the process. We use the term supervision within the diagram to represent formal supervision of any doctoral research projects, which we discuss in Chapter 7, but also to indicate the importance of guidance and support for studies of any type and scale. Supervision of doctoral research will support IPA researchers to articulate their research design and support the reflexive process. Chapter 7 explores the supervisory relationship and how supervision can support IPA social work projects from the perspectives of both supervisors and researchers. The authors will outline how essential supervision was to the example studies. A broader network of support can support IPA in social work. It is important to identify who can be part of your network of support. Who might be appropriate or helpful for guiding your study, or for supporting you during the process? Think about how this support differs from any other professional support that you have.

The early sections of the book outlined the importance of reflexivity and how this is a parallel of effective social work practice. This involves development of self-awareness, looking inwards and exploring what is happening in the research process from different angles. This can be a significant emotional experience (Ross 2017). Reflexivity needs to be an authentic aspect of the IPA approach to become aware of and manage our own emotions, ethics, boundaries and biases – it is the vehicle for bracketing. An integrated reflexive process can be transformative for researchers (Anzul et al. 1991) in terms of their own identity and development. Reflexivity also demonstrates transparency and the audit trail of data collection and analysis processes (Vicary et al. 2017).

Both authors used a journal to reflect on what was going on in their thought processes during the example studies. We will use some examples of extracts from these journals to highlight how they have helped work through issues in the research process. The following extract explored a turn in the choice of methodology:

> I have had my heart set on using action research and have started to be more and more uncomfortable with the fit of this. I intended to explore how we might improve workplace learning for social workers and became increasingly aware of the contested and diverse definitions of and meanings associated with what learning is for this professional group, and what this is in the workplace context. What remained foregrounded in any ideas I have is the position of the participants and a commitment to ensure they are positioned at the fore of the research in terms of the value of their experiences. A massive lightbulb moment has been thinking about if I were undertaking research with people using social work services, I would have firstly considered exploring their lived experiences therefore why would I not be doing this for social workers to understand more about what I do not yet understand. The process of supervision and cycle of reflection have really helped shift my thinking from a discomfort and dissonance with the original research strategy to consider the opportunity of a phenomenological study.
>
> Reflective extract A (Ferguson 2021: 218)

Gillian also used an audio diary to capture and acknowledge emotions and thoughts. This was effective in recording immediate responses to interviews once they had taken place and within the analysis phase whilst immersed in the data. In the same way that we might promote reflection in and for practice, trigger questions can help researchers develop their skills. Roller (2015) suggests that key questions about assumptions, values and emotions can support reflexivity as another parallel with social work professional development.

Some helpful reflective questions might include:

- What assumptions have I made?
- How has this affected the process, my interactions and the dialogue?
- What did I notice?
- What got in the way of my attention?
- How did I feel during, and after…?
- How did emotions affect what was going on?

You might want to use different questions that promote your reflexivity or feel that a more free-flow style of reflective journal would work for you. In the example of Sarah's study, she created a reflective journal within a qualitative software package. This worked well for Sarah as a way of reflecting but also enabling analysis. Additionally, the use of this, and especially the transparency it afforded, also contributed to the quality and validity (Vicary et al. 2017).

Conclusion

This chapter has provided a focus on the foundations for IPA social work research and has introduced a holistic model which can help inform your study design. It is important to have a clear focus for your study and to consider the context of this within the social work practice and policy context.

Summary points

- **Ethical foundations:** Make these clear in your research design and use reflexivity to the integrity of your study at all stages.
- **Refine your focus:** What do you want to explore, why does this matter and who will benefit? What do you want to understand? How is this connected to social work?
- **Lived experiences:** How will a focus on lived experiences help you in your sense-making quest?
- **Holistic process:** Remember the holistic process for IPA research in social work and consider how you are crafting your design.
- **Self-Awareness:** Identify the roles, interests and perspectives that you are bringing to your research. How do these influence your research and what might interfere?
- **Guiding your study:** Be clear on your plan for effective use of supervision and reflexivity. Consider who your research network of support will be.

This chapter has considered the foundations and focus of your social work research as you embark on your IPA journey. so Part 2 will now explore the methods which can sustain commitment to the three aspects of IPA: phenomenology, hermeneutics and idiography, and lead to effective social work IPA results.

Part **2**

Doing IPA Social Work Research

4 Research design: commitment to IPA methodology and methods

Chapter aims:

- to consider appropriate methods for your IPA social work study
- to explore how the integrated elements of IPA are woven into your design
- to explore data generation and collection approaches
- to connect your research design to the foundations and next steps.

Introduction

An effective IPA study involves designing and using methods that generate relevant, rich data as outlined in Part 1. Methods and procedures for gathering, managing and analysing this data build on the ethical foundations introduced as part of the holistic model for IPA social work research in Chapter 3. Essentially everything that you do within your research project to generate, gather or analyse your data is part of the methods and procedures. It is important that these are appropriate for IPA and interrelate. Smith et al. (2022) provide a comprehensive overview of IPA research procedures which includes practical activities to help shape your research; the authors recommend this as an essential reference volume if you are new to IPA. Strategies for getting and staying on track are an important part of the researcher's planning, reflection and review. Chapter 3 explored the focus and foundations for your study. This chapter continues the journey of designing IPA social work research using examples from the authors as illustrations.

Design choices for Phenomenology, Hermeneutics and Idiography

The integral components of IPA need to remain at the forefront of the study to retain commitment to the process. In general, the rigour of research demonstrates validity and reliability (Sarantakos 1993). Paley (2017) suggests that

phenomenological research approaches must differ from other forms of qualitative research in articulated clear and specific ways. Transparency of the
detailed procedures of data collection and analysis can support this articulation (Smith 2011a; Yardley 2000). Sensitivity to context, commitment and rigour
are principles identified by Yardley (2000) as equally important. Essentially
there needs to be a very clear fit between what has been happening backstage
(Chenail 1995) and the eventual presentation of the data. We will now explore
more about specific things to consider when designing your methods and procedures for IPA social work research.

Sample, research site and recruitment strategy

The issue of sample might seem straightforward for social work IPA research
and is a persisting dilemma for most researchers. First there is homogeneity; as
Smith et al. 2022 suggest, this homogeneity relates to the phenomena under
exploration and to other aspects such as the participants' contexts. The examples which we introduced in Chapter 3 include homogeneity, whereby the
researcher sought to understand the experience of a sample that undertakes
the same professional role, and the second being the experiences of social
workers learning in their workplace context. Participants are therefore selected
purposively to provide insight to the phenomenon in question and to have a
particular or idiographic perspective. Second there is size. Smith and colleagues
state that there is no right answer as to the question of numbers, depending as
this does on matters such as the richness of the case and the organisational
constraints in which the research is being undertaken. It is nonetheless true
that higher numbers do not necessarily mean 'better' data or findings in an IPA
study (Smith et al. 2022: 46–47). While Finlay (2011) suggests between three
and six participants are appropriate for an IPA sample, Smith suggests quality
over quantity as the primary consideration and a small number of participants
particularly if they are being interviewed more than once (Smith et al. 2009).
Dahlberg et al. (2008) reinforce that the exact number is not important in lifeworld research provided the reasons for the sample size are clear. Although a
small number of participants can be sufficient for IPA a larger sample is not
problematic, but attention to managing the volume of rich data and analysing
this in depth needs to be considered. The answer, if any, that does lie behind the
question of size is that it must afford the researcher the opportunity to undertake detailed analysis of the data. Ultimately it is important that you can justify
the sample size and have a rationale for why this is right for your research.
Reasons will include the kind of participants you need in terms of their lived
experiences of the same phenomenon and the richness of the data. Think about
who your participants might be. How will you define whether they have the
insight into the phenomenon you want to study and in what depth?

Once you have a clear focus for your research and have considered the
nature and size of the sample, you will be thinking about where you can recruit
appropriate participants. If you are exploring a local, practice-related phenomenon you might be an insider-researcher and already plan to recruit from within
a known organisation. Alternatively, you might be hoping to recruit participants

from a much wider geographic practice specialism or people who have been using specific social work services. Think about where the routes are that offer opportunities to share information about your research, and think about who any gatekeepers might be as discussed in Chapter 3. You may know of a professional network which is interested in the area that you are researching or explore whether there are overarching organisations where potential participants are involved. Many researchers have existing networks to draw on; however, this is not always the case, and either way it is important to ensure that you carefully consider where you are promoting your research. Think about the kind of data you are looking for and the participants you want to recruit. Many researchers use social media platforms and feeds to publicise their research and to seek participants. In other cases, it can be helpful for information to be circulated by relevant online networks which have an audience likely to include those who have the experience you seek. This is not always appropriate, and it is important to think about how this is managed ethically, and how you might respond to any posts related to your research in this public arena.

Before we go on to explore other methods and procedures more fully, Table 4.1 includes a summary of the data collection, sample and recruitment approaches taken by the authors in the example studies. You can see the sampling strategy from these studies in the first few sections of the table.

Both example studies have identified a sample strategy appropriate to the focus of their studies with participants who were likely to give an in-depth account of the phenomenon in question. Approaches to recruit participants have been selected which have been able to reach the appropriate population and in both cases use gatekeepers in organisations to facilitate dissemination of information. The profile of the eventual samples varied from the intention in both cases with less being involved in Example Study 1 and more in Example Study 2.

Sarah:

> The intention had been to recruit five of each of the eligible professionals: social workers, mental health nurses, occupational therapists and psychologists. It ended up that no psychologist had at that time been approved in the role. It was relatively easy to access social work participants, nurses less so and occupational therapists the most difficult. Just eight occupational therapists had trained at the time of accessing the sample. Of these, four were approached by the gatekeeper and two agreed to participate in the study.

Gillian:

> I was concerned that I wouldn't have enough rich data or participants might withdraw prior to the follow-up interview due to work demands or something. All those who took part in their initial interviews did, however, proceed. I decided it would be unethical to reject any of the interviews already undertaken after people had agreed to take part and offered their time. I interviewed 16 social workers resulting in a total of 32 interviews, so it was an incredible amount of data to be immersed in, and I kept wondering if it was maybe a bit too much.

Table 4.1 Summary of data collection methods and procedures

Summary of data collection methods and procedures in example studies	
Research questions	**Example Study 1:** What are the lived experiences of Approved Mental Health Professionals fulfilling their role?
	Example Study 2: What are the experiences of social workers learning in the workplace?
Sample	**Example Study 1:** Purposive, homogenous (in terms of approved mental health professional role). Participants who were all current approved mental health professionals who shared the same experience of undertaking assessments. Intention at outset to recruit five of each eligible profession: social workers; mental health nurses; occupational therapists and psychologists.
	Example Study 2: Purposive, homogenous (in terms of being social workers, employed in the setting who had been employed more than 2 years). Intention at outset to recruit 12 social workers and to interview them on more than one occasion.
Recruitment strategy	**Example Study 1:** In the first instance through a long-established network, liaison with gatekeeper who was contacted and who distributed information to potential participants. This was followed up with contact to representatives from relevant health trusts where practitioners had trained in the approved mental health professional role. Contacts in the trusts distributed study information and participants responded directly to the researcher.
	Example Study 2: Localised recruitment within one organisation in which there were ample suitable participants employed. Initial publicity and information distributed by gatekeeper within the organisation (Chief Social Work Officer) to all social work employees. Potential participants then contacted researcher directly.
Research site	**Example Study 1:** Nationwide (England) across services where participants were in practice in the approved mental health professional role.
	Example Study 2: Single local authority setting (Scotland)

(continued)

Table 4.1 (*Continued*)

Summary of data collection methods and procedures in example studies	
Participant profile	**Example Study 1:** Five social workers who had been an approved mental health professional (or its equivalent) from between 5 to over 15 years. Five nurses who had been in the role for between 1 and 3 years. Two occupational therapists who had been in the approved mental health professional role for 2 years.
	Example Study 2: Sixteen social workers who were currently working in one local authority site. A profile was mapped that showed participants had worked across local authority, third sector within UK and international settings. Practice was described in the study from diverse Children and Families, Adult Services and Justice Settings. Participants had been qualified for an average of 14 years spanning a range of 4 to 40 years. Five of the social workers held a practice educator qualification.
Data collection methods	**Example Study 1:** Individual interviews. Participants asked to draw a rich picture to trigger reflection and discussion of their experience of the approved mental health professional role and undertaking Mental Health Act assessments. Semi-structured interviews were used to develop discussion. Interviews audio recorded and transcribed by the researcher.
	Example Study 2: Individual interviews. Participants took part in an initial interview where a semi-structured interview was used. After the first interview, a verbatim transcript was prepared and sent to the participant in advance of a follow-up interview. Within the follow-up interview one open question was used, 'What sense did the social worker make of their experience?' Interviews audio recorded and transcribed by the researcher.

The example studies show very different sampling and recruitment strategies, however there is a clear rationale in each for who would offer insights into the phenomena under investigation. Within these examples there is also a clear connection and pathway between the intention of the studies and how participants will be recruited. It is crucial to map out recruitment considerations in advance in terms of the practicalities and the ethics of your approach. Getting this part of your study design right will set up the next steps for how you will generate and collect data.

Data collection

The most appropriate methods for IPA are those which afford rich, detailed first-person accounts of experience (Smith et al. 2022: 53). Individual interviews remain the most popular choice of data collection method for IPA studies, and qualitative research more generally; however, alternative and creative methods also are also increasingly used (Smith et al. 2022). Semi-structured and unstructured interviews are commonly used. Other methods can include for example focus groups, diaries and arts-based approaches. Remember that the function of your methods is to elicit rich description of lived experience and the sense this makes for your participants. Phenomenological interviews intend to 'contextualise… apprehend … and clarify the phenomenon' (Bevan 2014: 139). This is a reminder that being clear about the focus of what you want to explore is essential. Consider in what ways you are most likely to generate this type of data from the participants you will be recruiting. You might consider that a semi-structured interview, with a series of clustered questions, enables you to explore participants' experiences using prompts to probe for more depth (Gray 2014). Approaches to interviewing in IPA allow for deviation from set questions; however, it is vital that flexibility is managed, and you stay on track avoiding bias (Gray 2014). You seek to explore the structure and texture of a person's lifeworld. Designing questions that will reveal details of sensory experiences, sights, sounds, smells, tastes or touch as part of experiences might be part of the layers of description that lead to insights. Fundamentally, any method must allow participants the opportunity to tell their story by talking without constraint and in a reflective way.

In Example Study 1, Sarah used a semi-structured interview and use of rich pictures. Participants were asked to do a drawing of the phenomenon in question and to describe this during the interview. The drawing was used to elicit data and later to illustrate the findings. This is perhaps one of the more imaginative ways of collecting data to which Smith and colleagues refer and for which they also suggest methods that might access the chosen phenomena from more than one perspective or at more than one point in time (Smith et al. 2022: 53).

'Rich picture' is the name given to a drawing technique first used as part of a diagramming method: Soft Systems Methodology (Checkland 1980). Drawing, a term which refers to the process and the product, comes under the umbrella of visual research methods whose use is increasing in many areas of research (Theron et al. 2011) including applied research such as nursing (Kearney and Hyle 2004) and social work (Hus 2012). A rich picture has two purposes: to elicit a response about the phenomenon and to record this, pictorially, as participants are asked to draw a representation of the studied phenomenon. The rationale for its use in generating data in this way has been discussed more fully elsewhere (Matthews 2013), but in summary reasons include simplicity and tangibility; researchers need only provide a pen and paper and once drawn, the participant has something about which they can talk. Moreover, since the production of a drawing arguably uses different cognitive processes, its use can also provide an opportunity to access thoughts, feelings and emotions in other ways (Guillemin 2004; Kearney and Hyle 2004). To that end asking participants to draw in this instance was one way of eliciting meaning using unusual (to the participants) communication techniques and allowing them to further explore meaning which might otherwise have been latent. In Sarah's study, rich pictures were used to 'further enable the revelation of thoughts and feelings of the participants who were asked to talk about their drawing as part of the semi-structured interview' (Vicary 2017: 92).

Gillian also used semi-structured interviews, with carefully designed questions and possible prompts. An initial interview was undertaken and then a verbatim transcript provided to participants. A follow-up interview was then used to promote more in-depth exploration of participant's experiences and develop the sense-making process. These follow-up interviews posed only one question: 'What was interesting or important to the participant from their transcript?' to trigger discussion. Participants shared their reflective insights, and the researcher then followed up with anything that they had noticed which seemed important from the original accounts. For example, if participants had used metaphors, or language that seemed to convey aspects of the essence of their experience, this was followed up. Both researchers reflected on their chosen data collection methods as having clearly generated the type of data that they sought.

Conducting IPA interviews

Whatever your intended data collection method, it is important to negotiate effective ethical boundaries. This will include reiterating the parameters of the session, and how data will be recorded, stored and managed. You should be mindful of the need for ongoing 'specific oral consent for unanticipated and emerging issues' (Smith et al. 2009: 53). If you are an insider-researcher, as discussed in Chapter 3, reclarify your role as a researcher in the process and highlight how any sensitive issues will be managed should they arise.

At the initial stages of an interview, it may be that you are doing quite a bit of talking to set things up as a foundation for discussion. You can helpfully foreground your intention to give voice to the lifeworld (Larkin et al. 2006). This can help build an interview environment which focuses on individual lived experiences. It is important that participants know that this is the type of research you are doing, and this will ideally have been explained clearly in your recruitment information. Sarah's experience of asking participants to draw meant that she had built the interview environment through explaining what a rich picture is and what participants needed to do. Her first question was 'please can you describe your drawing', and often this was the only question needed. For all participants having the focus of the drawing was helpful in easing the flow of the interview.

Setting up the interview

Key things to cover:

- the purpose of the research
- ethical approval, safeguards and revisit consent
- nature of interview and/or creative method (s)
- use of audio recording for production of transcripts
- nature of data analysis
- ability for participant withdrawal
- anonymity, boundaries, confidentiality, fitness to practise, whistleblowing and data protection
- reminder of contacts regarding any concerns about the research.

Setting up the interview allows participants to settle into the session and you might introduce a fairly general question to begin, allowing them to choose where to start from in their accounts of lived experience. The dialogue will then shift at this stage from you speaking to actively listening in detail to what is said. It is essential that the prominent voice in the interview is that of the participant.

Remote data gathering

It can be easy to imagine how to gather data when physically present with people who are participating in your research. It is now, however, increasingly common for research interviews to be carried out online. We suggest that rather than considering this as a completely separate way of undertaking research, attention to the essential components of the data collection can help support on – or offline methods. It is vital to think about the safeguards of remote audio, video or art/text-based methods. Setting up a safe environment for the process means ensuring sufficient details are included for participants, and considering the support that they might need to take part. If a participant is taking part from their own home, is the environment conducive or safe to do so? How will participants be supported, if necessary, before or after the interviews? Attention to the devices and online platforms that will be used is also important. Will participants have access to appropriate devices? What contingency measures can be planned for in case of technical difficulties on the day? Ways of communicating online or by telephone are also different, so it is important to think about these in advance and integrate them into your study design. There are excellent examples of effective studies which have used remote methods for data collection, where these issues have been considered.

Interviewing skills

Active listening is the most important aspect of the interview: picking up on what the participant has said, paraphrasing, clarifying and noting any nuanced language or metaphor that provides insight into the lifeworld. As you begin to listen and respond, you will be trying to move to deeper description. Using prompts and clarifying questions will be helpful at this stage, in a similar way that social work practice will use advanced communication skills to listen and develop understanding. An interesting comparison can be drawn between skilful approaches to social work practice, such as Motivational Interviewing (MI) and IPA interviewing techniques. First, MI techniques include active listening, careful paraphrasing and developing depth in eliciting information about a person's experiences and perspectives. Second, MI skills promote the person's understanding or interpretation of their experiences through them learning what [they] think as they hear themselves talk (Miller and Rollnick 2013). Choosing what to pick up on, respond to or clarify is a judgement on the part of the interviewer. If you are coming to IPA research with social work practice experience, think about the knowledge and skills that can be transferred to your research role to strengthen the micro-skills of interviewing. You may also want to read the debate in Chapter 2 which discusses the fit between social work skills and social work research skills.

Holding silence or managing heightened emotions are other important skills that can be drawn from a counselling approach to practice that serve you well in research interviews. These help you avoid a premature focus on issues before the participant has had a chance to develop their own thinking and can also help you respond to the emotional context of the research interview. Providing the questions is worth considering; this demonstrates openness in the research process and allows the participant to be aware of the scope of the questions. The human exchange in the interview is essential for IPA and an important area for reflecting on managing self and the process (Ross 2017). Interviewing style and skills are therefore very important.

The importance of your questions

Smith et al. (2022) provide detailed information about shaping questions for IPA studies. The use of classic open questions are the vehicle for IPA interviews: *How did that make you feel?* and *Can you tell me more about that?* (Smith et al. 2022: 61), but these need to be sensitively and authentically employed. Table 4.2 summarises the questions used in the example studies.

Sarah's example study concerns a 'pearl' after Smith (2011c) in which a small part of her data formed a pivotal part of the corpus of her research analysis. One of her participants drew and described what she as the analyst later interpreted as pull: the active use of dissonance, whereby the rich picture – the meaning made of it by the participant and in turn the analyst – constitutes a different understanding of the part emotion plays in the fulfilment of the approved mental health professional role (Vicary 2021: 13).

Closing the interview: things to think about

Closing the interview gives you the opportunity to check how this has gone and clarify information about what happens next. Checking if the interview

Table 4.2 Interview questions used in example studies

Examples from Gillian's interview questions	Examples from Sarah's interview questions
Tell me about your experiences of learning as a social worker through your work activities.	Can you tell me about you as an approved mental health professional? (Prompts: your professional background? How long have you done this role? Approximately how many assessments have you undertaken? What do you believe are the most important aspects of the AMHP role? Can you describe any aspect in detail? Are there any aspects that you think are more important?)
Are there any particularly vivid experiences you can describe to me?	
What particular feelings, sounds, smells and objects were associated with that experience?	Can you please talk me through the rich picture which you created? (Prompts: please describe the picture. Did anything surprise you when you were drawing it? Is there anything in the picture that you found difficult to portray? Is there anything that didn't come up that they were expecting to come up?)
How has this experience influenced you as a social worker?	
What does learning in your workplace mean to you?	I would like to find out more about your experience of being an AMHP (Prompts: how do you feel? With whom do you consult and why?)
Questions included a focus around the sensory experiences of social workers, in examples of their learning to tune into the lifeworld.	Questions drawn from the rich pictures produced at the start of the interview and focus on what it is like to be an approved mental health professional.
The focus of the study is on the phenomenon of *learning* which is clear in the questions.	The schedule has a series of possible prompts should they be needed to promote discussion.
Questions allowed participants to describe whatever came to mind about the phenomenon.	
Prompts and clarifying questions were used to stay on track with the exploration.	
Elaboration and deeper description were encouraged.	
Any recurring points or ideas expressed that seemed important to the participant were highlighted.	

questions have been clear and whether there is any other feedback on the practical arrangements can help you review your approach. You can also clarify the process after the interview. This might include any information about how the transcriptions will be managed, who will see the data and how the research findings will be used. Simple as it seems, it is also essential to remember to thank participants for their time. Making sure to add these notes on your interview schedule can help you remember to do so.

Reviewing where you are in the holistic process

The next steps of your research involve carefully managing data and attention to the analysis process. Wherever you are in the process of your research it is a good idea to review your plans or progress so far. Are you gathering the type of data you hoped for? If undertaking a large scale or doctorate study, it is usual to test out the methods that you will be using for data collection. This will enable you to make any alterations that maximise the potential for gathering phenomenological data. It is also helpful if you can reflect on the shape of the research and how the intrapersonal processes are going. Taking stock of how you are feeling as a researcher and reviewing your reflective notes should be integrated in the whole process. The analysis stage of IPA is inevitably a complex process due to the nature of the data and the hermeneutic, sense-making quest. It is to this analysis that this book now turns in Chapter 5.

Summary points

- **Methods matter:** Have you selected methods that will generate rich phenomenological data?
- **Lived experiences:** Check that your questions will get to the heart of individual experiences.
- **Holistic process:** Remember the holistic process for IPA research in social work and consider how you are crafting your design, building on the ethical foundations.
- **Self-awareness:** Think about how your interests and skills are influencing your research and whether this is helpful or otherwise.
- **Guiding your study:** Use your network of support, supervision and reflexive approach to evaluate your design and progress with data collection. Is your research on track to explore your social work focus?

This chapter has explored how you can build on a clear focus for your research with carefully selected methods and procedure to retain commitment to IPA. Chapter 5 will now continue to explore the analysis process sustaining commitment to your social work focus and the three aspects of IPA: Phenomenology; Hermeneutics and Idiography.

---

5 A sense-making quest

Chapter aims:

- to position analysis as an integrated aspect of your IPA social work research
- to provide a pathway to arrive at interpreted accounts of lived experience
- to explore the hermeneutic sense-making quest
- to discuss commitment to phenomenology, idiography and hermeneutics in your analysis
- to consider how to confidently justify findings.

Introduction

In Chapter 3 we introduced the holistic model for IPA social work research, and important messages about designing an effective study that will generate sufficient rich data that can be analysed. Rather than a distinct and separate element of research, sense-making is integral to the process as you gather data and become immersed in accounts of lived experience. Although this will be a unique experience for each researcher, a clear approach and audit trail of the analysis process are essential. In this context, clear does not mean simple; the analysis phases of your research can be daunting, but understanding how to remain committed to the three components of IPA can help you stay on track.

Researchers can feel apprehensive about delving into data in any research project. The volume and nature of data can mean that researchers feel overwhelmed about what counts as important, and who decides this. Doing justice to the lived experiences of the people who have shared their accounts with you is central to the process. As with the other stages of your project, justification of your choices and decisions about methods is important. Making defensible decisions is fundamental to social work practice, and doing so within the research process requires a similar approach to weighing up options and being able to justify what you do. Chapter 7 will explore defending your research in terms of doctoral studies, but it is important to be able to justify and account for your decisions in any well-designed project. Ultimately, the aim is to arrive at interpreted accounts of lived experience that stay true to the person as revealed in the data.

Steps to sense-making

We describe the analysis phase of your study as a sense-making quest which integrates the practical and intellectual processes that you are engaged in during IPA. As with many other forms of research, analysis is an iterative and inductive cycle (Smith 2007). Qualitative research often poses many questions about what has been found out, what counts as important, what counts as a theme and ultimately what new knowledge has been generated. Smith and colleagues outline suggested steps in the IPA sense-making process. While clear steps are outlined, there is no 'prescriptive account' and there can be 'healthy flexibility' (Smith et al. 2022: 75). We do not attempt to reiterate the details offered by Smith et al. in respect of analysis and highly recommend those new to IPA to familiarise themselves with the origins and development of the approach alongside the guidance offered. We will, of course, highlight specific aspects of the steps proposed by Smith et al. and set these within our discussion in this chapter. We suggest elements in Figure 5.1 that integrate different phases of the sense-making quest in IPA social work research. The central steps are drawn from the analysis process identified in Smith et al. (2022), which are held and supported by integrated reflexivity and other elements that form the overall sense-making process.

Figure 5.1 A sense-making quest

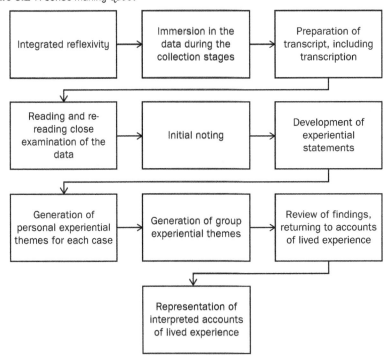

These elements are now explored, and we propose that they are a dynamic continuation of your project building on the data collection stages and bring your research full circle in relation to the holistic model introduced in Chapter 3.

Integrated reflexivity

Analysing your data is a unique and personal part of the sense-making quest and we have positioned this as the first element in the analysis process. It is, in fact, a constant part of the process rather than a separate step and referred to in the earlier chapters of the book. If the analysis process feels messy, it may be so for a reason. If findings do not initially seem clear, it may be because they are not yet understood. Your relationship with the data may be intense, and your reflexive work in managing your own emotions, reactions and interpretation are central to the process. Make a plan that will work for you about managing the reflexive process as you continue your journey.

Delving into the data

During data collection, the active listening process, clarifying and checking understanding is part of your sense-making. Once you have gathered data, there will be various ways that you begin to become immersed in the accounts of lived experience. If you have audio recorded interviews for example, you might listen to these again and notice things that sound important and be aware of how you are beginning to make sense of your participant's sense-making.

Developing robust and accurate verbatim transcripts from the data is essential for IPA and is most effective if this is undertaken by the researcher directly. Preparing transcripts does take a lot of time but allows you to spend time with the detail of the accounts of lived experience and stay close to the data. It is you who has been present in the data collection event so only you who can attest to the accuracy of the transcript. A well-prepared transcript is integral to your sense-making quest; it is vital that these are not 'tidied up' (Poland 1995: 302) but should capture non-verbal aspects, such as gestures or emotions that seem important. For example, one of Sarah's participants was particularly taken aback when they described their drawing as they had placed the service user at the edge of the picture albeit protected by a line depicting safety. Their value base was one of always keeping the person in the centre, hence the shock. They 'justified' such a discrepancy by suggesting that the actual process of dealing with the person was the relatively easy part, but as they were surrounded by other matters such as resource constraints and pressures of time the service user was placed in this way to separate and protect. In another example, Gillian captured the nature of a social worker's description of showing physical movement back and forward when they were recounting an interaction with a child: 'I think you've showed several times when you've been speaking about it, you've almost been back and forward with all the motion of that interaction' (Ferguson 2021: 67).

In a different example, the expression of emotion is captured in the transcript because it has been picked up in the interview and the transcript details that the participant is 'smiling and lighting up' (Ferguson 2021: 55) which has been reflected back to them in the dialogue. This is an example of how something important in the participant's experience is captured in the transcript, stemming from information presented non-verbally. Attention to these non-verbal aspects of the interviews enabled the researcher to acknowledge these as part of lived experience during data collection. Having a record of these allows the detail to be included in the interview transcript. In this way it is possible to capture gestures, pauses, laughter or other details as part of preparation for analysis. How dialect is represented and managed within the transcript and subsequent sense-making is another issue to consider when you are working on your research.

Researchers who are recording using online platforms, or software that generates automatic transcripts from text, are still likely to have to amend these and make checks on their accuracy. While it can be tempting to take what might be perceived as shortcuts, time spent at this point will be welcomed in the later stages of your analysis which is 'an iterative and fluid process of engagement with the transcript' (Smith et al. 2022: 77). This advice poses challenges for teams of researchers where there might be different people undertaking data collection and transcription and involved in analysis. In a separate research study (Wiles and Vicary 2019) where the analysis was undertaken by two people, a decision was taken to undertake analysis separately in the first instance and to then come together to discuss what had been found and to compare (and contrast). It will be important to think about how these aspects of the research can be managed in such cases.

Systematic management of the data

Although an exciting part of the research journey, managing the volume of phenomenological data generated by your study needs to be carefully planned and monitored. This can help you to avoid becoming overwhelmed with the data as you delve into this. While Vagle (2018) touches on a fear of computer-assisted software this need not detract from the analysis process. Sarah has effectively used a computer software tool first, as mentioned in Chapter 3, to manage data and embed reflexive notes throughout the analysis phase. In essence, Sarah imported her transcripts and photographs of the rich pictures into the tool and used its functions to show quality and validity through an audit trail (Vicary et al. 2017). In addition, with linked memos housing her reflections on the data and the process, she was able to bracket out her preconceptions – including in discussions with her supervisors – a process to which we will return in Chapter 7.

In contrast, Gillian decided to manage data differently in her study; she tested out using several types of software but found that she was able to explore the data easier in printed and written note form. Data nonetheless was stored in a careful, organised system which could keep track and ensure all documentation was secure. Whatever you choose to do, think about how you can plan effectively in advance and if something is not working for you, adapt to maximise your opportunity to become immersed in the data. Whether you use computer-assisted software or otherwise, in qualitative research it is you who does the analysis.

Staying immersed – sense-making cycles

We have considered delving into the data but now turn to staying immersed to continue your sense-making. We describe this as sense-making cycles as it is non-linear and fluid and foregrounds the interpretive element of IPA social work research. A caution is highlighted by Smith et al., which is in attending too much to the descriptive without the interpretative in the process (Smith et al. 2022: 106). Moving from the whole of the transcript to different parts then returning to the whole is a component of phenomenological research, including IPA, which can flow naturally through the sense-making process. It is important to be clear about this as an integral component and to be able to show how this is built into your analysis and explication of experiential statements.

A person is retrospectively reflecting on their lived experience as a 'flesh and blood' human being (van Manen 2016: 14). It is hugely important that attention is therefore paid to the embodied, sensory experience to really get to the heart of what a person's lifeworld is like. We briefly introduced the lifeworld existentials (van Manen) in Chapter 1 which help us understand and tune in to the multiple layers of lived experience. Corporeality, how we experience the world in relation to both having and being a body, is therefore central to understanding and interpreting your data. This is a helpful reminder to consider what you notice in the data that helps you make sense of the lived experiences as they are expressed. Integrated reflexivity supports you to also be aware of your own physical and emotional reactions. Think about how and where the physical and emotional parts of experience manifest and how they form part of the phenomenon that you are researching.

Phenomenological research is to evoke understandings through language. However, Todres (2007) states that language cannot fully summarise the lifeworld and highlights the role of the lived body. He argues that the body is part of the world, and through which the person gains perspective and reflects on their experience of being in that world. This is closely linked with the perspectives of others in positioning the body as intuitively present in any act of understanding the structure of experience in the world and the link to tacit wisdom (Merlau-Ponty 1945; Dahlberg et al. 2008; van Manen, 2016). It is essential therefore to take account of the experience of the lived body, and this extends across and beyond our senses. Phenomenology is for Todres (2007) embodied enquiry.

In our approach to sense-making, we have clustered the steps outlined by Smith et al. (2022) within the process. You might already have begun listening, reading and re-reading your transcripts. It is essential to engage in a close examination of the data. You might also have made some initial notes about

Figure 5.2 Initial noting on transcript (Ferguson 2021: 59)

your thoughts. It is vital that you do not prematurely decide what a theme might be at this stage, instead noting your thoughts, reflections and reactions as you work through the material. The process of analysis undertaken by Sarah is depicted in a screen shot (Vicary et al. 2017: 555–58). Figure 5.2 shows some initial notes on a transcript from Gillian's study.

At this time as a researcher Gillian has just highlighted striking aspects of the lived experience and made some summary notes in the right-hand column. She has underlined some phrases that seemed important from her understanding at that point of immersion in the data. Notes were then made in the right-hand column of transcripts including those that were descriptive or general; those that were linguistic (highlighted on the text) or where metaphors were used to describe experience; and comments that were more conceptual (underlined) about the ideas presented. This system for noting within IPA (Smith et al. 2009) is seen on the following extract of Kathleen's transcript in Figure 5.3.

It is possible to see the difference in these styles of noting for the same transcript extract at different points of immersion in the sense-making cycle. Gillian also used a practical approach to looking at the whole of the lived experience by moving from the parts deconstructed on the transcript to get a sense of how the

Figure 5.3 Transcript extract with disciplined notes (Ferguson 2021: 63)

Emergent themes	Original Transcript	Exploratory notes Descriptive (plain text) Linguistic (highlighted) Conceptual (underlined)
Sense of self in journey	**Kathleen** So I went from that into an actual locality childcare team, in	Journey
	XXXXXXXX and oh hoh (laughing) so that was fun! I knew some of the workers	
Culture shock	from having the young people in the residential units so some of them, but that	Expectations and reality
	was a complete again other culture shock this is the way a team in , I don't	Culture shock
	know what I thought I was going to as a social work team, I'm going to be in a	
The role of mavericks	team of social workers with a manager, it's all going to be organised and what	Role of maverick role of dissenters?
Sense of place	I'm meant to be doing and when I got there it was eh, what I later discovered	Risky places
Isolation	that I didn't know any better so I think XXXXXXXXXX is, but I later discovered	
An assault on all the senses	was probably a bit maverick, the way workers went about things. The building	Elements of what comprises the place –
	itself was really risky, they didn't have even, I know it's knocked down now the	dog – people-glass-door-substances -no
Feeling blind	building but, more lately when I visited they put in a wee bit of an entrance bit	computers-no natural light
	to prevent people from just walking straight? It was like a pre door kind of thing,	
	that didn't exist when I was there, so I arrived and got told there's your room	
Feeling and being unsafe	and it was right beside the front door and I remember sitting at the desk writing	
	and turning round and a massive big dog right behind my arm, came wandering	
	in and its owner then subsequently came wandering in and it ehm severely	An assault on all the senses
	affected by substances so there was, it was dark and I think it was winter when	Feeling blind
	I went (laughing), so it was winter, it was dark, the windows were all, it's on the	Embodied experiences?
	ground floor, but the window let no light in and they got so fed up replacing the	Other people not being there and the
	glass they had put this sort of Perspex you couldn't see out, so there was nae	influence of this
Feeling unsafe	natural light, no computers, there was only one computer in the office and that	Feeling unsafe
Absence of others	belonged to the admin worker and if you needed anything typed you had to	Interviewer trying to check the learning
Presence of others	write it by hand and hand it to them, all your case notes were hand written and	within the experience
	so it was I just felt it was an assault on all the senses	Interview focus and refocus on the
	G That's interesting	learning aspects of the experience
	Kathleen Just everything, I felt unsafe, but it looked like everybody else was	The role of the maverick in influencing
The maverick	getting on with it so this must be the way it is, ehm hardly saw my manager, I'd	learning

Figure 5.4 Seeing the whole (Ferguson, 2021: 62)

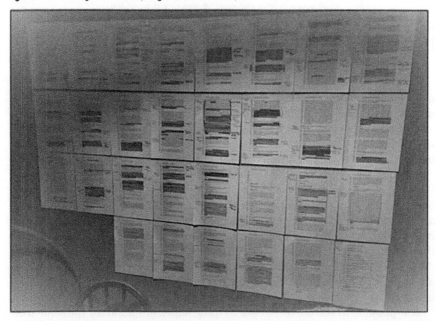

bigger picture made sense. Figure 5.4 is a photograph of the whole of the transcripts from Kathleen's interview which Gillian pinned to a wall.

Pinning all the transcript to a wall in this way enabled Gillian to engage in whole-part-whole analysis of Kathleen's lived experience, thereby retaining commitment to the hermeneutic aspect of the research. Vagle highlights that phenomenological research approaches share a 'commitment to a whole-part-whole analysis' (Vagle, 2018: 108). He describes the importance of acknowledging 'moments in relation to the whole' (p.108). Van Manen describes the 'shuttlecock' movement of the hermeneutic circle (van Manen 2014:10). Although this was a lengthy and immersive process, considering the data in this way helped Gillian have confidence in the eventual themes which emerged for each participant. If you have used individual interviews to collect data, it is usual to explore each case in turn before moving to the next (Smith et al. 2022: 78). This retains commitment to the idiographic aspect of IPA.

You might decide on a different process for noting, but it is important to have a clear strategy of what you are looking for to retain the focus on the phenomenon under exploration. Having a clear audit trail of your analysis process will include how you have approached the data at this stage. The analysis process can feel overwhelming at first, and sometimes remain so. At other times you might feel excited, confused, elated or any other combination of responses in relation to the process itself or anything that you are discovering in the data. This is all completely normal for an IPA study and the sense-making quest. Trust the process, don't rush to prematurely identify findings and ensure that you return to the data to confirm your discoveries throughout the analysis stage.

Development of experiential statements

In Smith et al. (2009) emergent themes were identified for each participant after close reading and initial noting. Smith et al. now suggest 'constructing experiential statements' which 'reflect not only the participant's original words but also the analyst's interpretation' (Smith et al. 2022: 86). In this way, you need to have spent time immersed in the data shifting in the whole-part-whole process to identify key statements that help convey components of the lived experience. In Figure 5.3, these are noted in the left-hand column, albeit labelled emergent themes in that study. Experiential statements are therefore powerful parts of the phenomenon as experienced. It can be daunting to decide what is emerging at this part of your research project, as you might think everything is important and it can be difficult to know what to select and what not to use. You are essentially making a judgement based on your interpretation of the participants' sense-making that stays true to their experience. You have been immersed in and continued a dialogue with the data as you make sense of the participant's sense-making. Nonetheless, making a decision can still be difficult so the guiding rules are: to consider why you are identifying an experiential statement; what is this based on; whether you can justify this; what the evidence is that leads you to know that this is important. Confidently deciding what is a theme in qualitative research can be a common dilemma. In phenomenology, van Manen suggests that 'a theme is the form of capturing the phenomenon one tries to understand'. Themes describe an aspect of the structure of lived experience and 'give shape to the shapeless' (van Manen 2014: 88). Van Manen highlights that phenomena are usually 'highly elusive' and the researcher 'must be able to maintain an almost unreasonable faith in the power of language to make intelligible and understandable what always seems to lie beyond language' (van Manen 2014: xviii).

Arriving at interpreted accounts of lived experience

In their first edition Smith et al. clustered 'emergent themes' to form 'superordinate themes' (Smith et al. 2009: 97). The terminology proposed in the second edition has shifted to 'personal experiential statements' that are organised or clustered to form 'personal experiential themes (PETS)' and 'group experiential themes' (GETS) (Smith et al. 2022: 76). They acknowledge that researchers may be using the original terms but recommend using the new. In effect, the aim is the same: to discover, reveal, interpret and represent lived experience of a phenomenon through 'reflective engagement' with the data (Smith et al. 2021: 77). This retains commitment to the phenomenological aspects of IPA social work research. Clustering experiential statements also involves your decisions about how to do so. As with all other decisions, you should consider and note the rationale for clustering. You could be faced with a large number of experiential statements or a smaller number of these depending on your data. The main aim is to stay close to the lived experience and trust the process.

Smith et al. (2022) offer suggestions for clustering based on numeration, similarity, polarisation or other connections. They suggest that IPA researchers can identify other means to cluster and that this 'need not be prescriptive' nor are approaches 'mutually exclusive' (Smith et al. 2009: 96), highlighting that researchers should select what fits for them in looking for patterns and connections between themes. In the example study, Gillian clustered according to Smith et al. (2009), by:

- abstraction where themes that seemed alike were put together
- subsumption where an emergent theme was identified itself as a superordinate theme, because of its status in relation to the experience and bringing together a number of other related themes
- polarisation where any oppositional relationships between emergent themes were present
- contextualisation where there was a reason to connect elements or emergent themes in relation to the narrative or, for example, specific events within the individual experience
- and finally, numeration where there was an indication through the frequency of emergent themes or ideas that this was important as part of the lived experience.

An initial clustering or organisation can then be refined as you bring your interpretative lens to the process. It is surprising how many ways your sense starts to emerge as you review, sort and consider the data.

Gillian noted specific details and quotes that were connected to these clusters, usually related to linguistic comments identified in the transcripts which helped convey the meaning interpreted by the participant and researcher. Importantly, Vagle stresses that 'sometimes a single statement, from one participant at one moment in time is so powerful that it needs to be amplified' (Vagle 2018: 109). Smith himself refers to this as a pearl or gem (Smith 2011c). This was the case for both Sarah and Gillian in their studies where powerful examples of the phenomenon under study shone through single statements.

A continual challenge throughout sense-making is not to oversimplify people's experiences although these are often presented in a list or table form. We have explored how visual methods can help give more detail and nuance of lived experience in Chapter 6. It is helpful to keep remembering the three aspects of IPA in your sense-making journey. A surprising number of researchers retain a focus on idiography and phenomenology, but the sense-making double hermeneutic process is neglected. Although always complex, and usually messy, tracking how you are attending to the whole-part-whole sense-making process is vital. IPA social work research is always dealing with the 'reflective interpretation, experience-sensitive understanding, the textuality of meaning and humanistic impulses' (van Manen 2016: xi). Reflect on where you have arrived and consider if the PETS do justice to the experience of your participant.

Generation of group experiential themes

Once you have worked through each individual case in turn, most IPA social work research will be looking to generate Group Experiential Themes, GETS (Smith et al. 2022: 76). You are likely to have noticed possible connections as you worked through the individual accounts of lived experience and made a note of things that struck you during that stage of the journey. It is important to acknowledge what you have noticed within the reflexive process then turn with disciplined attention to make sense of a 'cross-case analysis' rather than provide generalised findings (Smith et al. 2022: 100). Within the cross-case analysis Smith et al. consider exploring convergence and divergence within cases as one way into this part of the sense-making quest. There will be many other ways that strike you of beginning to explore and organise what you see across your individual PETS that can demonstrate understanding and meaning about the phenomenon under study.

In Gillian's example study, she wrote all individual themes on sticky note sheets and ordered them to form the clusters. By this stage she felt confident in what the nature of these individual aspects of experience were as part of the whole of the individual's lived experience. This was not a simple process but reflected the whole-part-whole process of analysis again. Specific ideas and quotes that had seemed important were also viewed. Smith et al. (2009) suggest recording the quotes in a spreadsheet for larger sample sizes so that these can be used to represent unique nuances but share higher order qualities. Gillian used a detailed spreadsheet to record all themes and to track the rationale for these and any changes made. This proved to be important to manage the volume of data, provide an audit trail, note changes in themes and record what each theme comprised. Gillian also recorded which of the social workers' individual themes had led to the formation of the group theme. In doing so she was able to easily find evidence that supported and illuminated the phenomenon.

Identifying GETS strongly involves bringing your interpretative role into the analysis process and to begin looking at what might be key emergent themes for the whole group. You are continuing to work within the sense-making cycles of whole-part-whole analysis, considering whether any themes help understand or illuminate the overall sense or essence of lived experience.

Summary points

- **Take time:** Don't rush analysis or prematurely identify personal experiential statements.
- **Lived experiences:** Maintain a strong, orientated focus on the phenomenon.
- **Sense-making:** Remember the whole-part-whole process in the hermeneutic circle.
- **Integrated reflexivity:** Attend to the reflexive process to support sense-making and manage self.

This chapter has explored how analysis is at the heart of IPA social work research, intricately connected to the rich data generated in the earlier stages of a project. Understanding the hermeneutic sense-making process and staying true to lived experiences is a thread running through successful IPA research. In Chapter 6, we consider the final two stages of Figure 5.1: how you can most effectively represent your findings and how to review the integrated elements of your IPA social work research.

6 Making a difference in social work through IPA research

Chapter aims:

- to consider how IPA social work findings can be represented
- to review the integrated aspects of IPA social work research
- to confirm the position of your findings in the knowledge landscape
- to explore how you can maximise the impact of your study for social work practice.

Introduction

We have explored the challenges of analysis in the previous chapter, and the process of developing confidence in your findings. This chapter now explores the next adventure – how your findings can be represented. The chapter will also highlight how you can reflect on your research project using the holistic model to review the integrated components. Now that you have come full circle in your project, the chapter encourages you to identify the position of the new knowledge that your study has generated within the social work landscape. Finally, the chapter will also discuss steps to maximise the impact of your research for social work practice.

The challenges of representing interpreted accounts of lived experience

Throughout the book we have explained the multiple layers of complexity involved in researching lived experience, the role of interpretation in IPA and paying close attention to the details for an effective study. The concept of research mindedness as a central embedded aspect of social work practice has continued to develop within the profession. This is explicit in the expectations of social workers across their career stages, embedded in social work education and continuing professional learning. No matter how small-scale your IPA study has been, there will be learning from the interpreted accounts of lived experience. Representation of your findings needs to reveal the interpreted accounts of lived experience in a way that stays true to the idiographic, phenomenological and hermeneutic process. Finding a way to show the nuances of your findings takes careful thought; however, you can convey this detail with care and creativity.

One way of reflecting on your findings is to ask, 'What have I really found out?'. This leads you to being very clear about the nature and summary of the findings. Reflecting on the origins and motivation of your study can be helpful as this reorientates you back to the focus of your research questions. You might have answered these clearly and can structure the findings into a simple framework that follows the ideas you set out to explore. In other studies, it will be less clear how to organise the findings to clearly communicate these to others.

It is important to include description and ensure the interpretative element is clear in your accounts of lived experience. An effective IPA social work research study will communicate the findings and then connect to a discussion about what these mean for practice and further study. Representing the complexity of lived experience is a real challenge. Thinking about how to summarise the information for other people to read inevitably means reducing details. You should consider what the essential aspects of your findings are and how can you convey these through description, examples and discussion. If you are writing up an academic thesis, there may be an expected format for your findings. In many cases you will have to decide what to include and how to do so. One of the most important aspects of your findings is how these can be represented in a way which stays true to the lived experiences of the people who have participated in your study. Showing sensitivity and respect in the way that you present accounts of lived experiences is one of the ethical components of an effective study that models social work values.

You might also have to consider if there are other ethical dilemmas in what and how you share. For example, might there be unintended consequences of the findings for social work, or the participants? How can you mitigate against these without compromising the integrity of your research? A well-designed study will have considered the potential ethical dilemmas from the outset but there are always surprises, so your reflexivity and use of your support network remain essential.

The ways that Sarah and Gillian chose to represent their findings in the example studies are very different, and we now explore these.

Representing the lived experience of approved mental health professionals

In this example, Sarah presented a discussion of the themes that had been discovered. She introduced, summarised and explored each of these themes in turn, using examples from different people's experience, verbatim extracts from interviews and examples of participants' rich pictures. The discussion of the different themes is developed to build a detailed case of the complex lived experience of the approved mental health professional (AMHP) role. Use of the verbatim extracts links the discussion clearly to the data from which the themes are drawn. Rich pictures, either in whole or excerpts thereof, were used to illustrate. A summary of each theme was also used at the end of the discussion of each theme to consolidate the researcher's interpretation. Of the various findings that have since been published from Sarah's doctoral study, one example concerns the theme of abandonment and sabotage. Upon signing a medical recommendation, AMHPs reported that doctors would leave the AMHP alone with the person who was liable to detention, regardless of any risk this might pose. This abandonment was encapsulated in a play on words that was made clear when one AMHP described the process as 'role over' and which Sarah as the analyst interpreted as 'roll over', a 'mistake' that was rectified by the excerpt of the rich picture. This seeming play on words also, however, illustrated that AMHPs in turn sabotaged this abandonment by, for example, refusing to undertake the administrative tasks the doctors had tried to assign. This subtle use of power between professionals involved in the same task yet with different functions is represented by this finding (Vicary et al. 2019). A second example which has been described, also in Chapter 4, concerns a different understanding of the use of emotion in fulfilment of the AMHP role in which it emerged that using dissonant emotions simultaneously in order to fulfill their role was a particular skill represented by the data as hovering (Vicary 2021).

Representing the lived experiences of social workers' learning in the workplace

In this example study, Gillian chose to develop a visual diagram to encapsulate the lived experiences of each individual participant in the study. This diagram was the picture of a web which linked the themes for the individual and conveyed that these were woven together by multiple threads and connections to form their lived experience of learning in the workplace as a social worker. Gillian used these diagrams to present part of the findings, followed by a discussion of the individual participant using verbatim extracts to support this. An example of the visual web is shown in Figure 6.1.

Subsequent discussion then included highlighting any major aspects of the encapsulated experience to bring these alive for the reader. In the example from Figure 6.1, central ideas about survival were discussed as Danny used a *sink or swim* metaphor throughout her interviews, connected closely with experiencing social work as an extraordinary job. The job had created *intrapersonal conflict* between Danny's private and professional life. Danny identifies learning as 'all-encompassing', 'every day' in 'small fragments of time' (Ferguson 2021: 136). Learning through the senses had supported Danny to learn how to practise, using her senses in relation to complex assessment work and intuitive wisdom so a verbatim quote was used to illustrate this in the representation of findings:

Figure 6.1 A visual web of lived experience Ferguson (2021: 137)

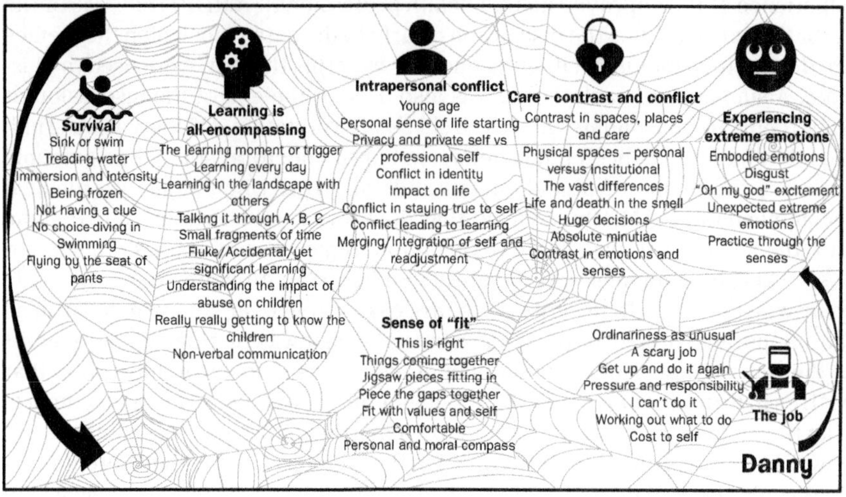

You have to think through your senses when working with people who don't verbally communicate. I think for me now, thinking about domestic violence, parental substance misuse, what children's lived experiences are, a lot of that comes through your senses. You can't pin it down to what you know, to what you see, it's what you feel, what you smell all these different things and you know from the research and things they're just as, if not more, important than some of the bigger grandiose stuff.

Ferguson (2021: 139)

This method of representation was selected in the research to convey the idiographic and phenomenological result of the hermeneutic cycle. After each social worker's experience had been presented, Gillian created a visual web which encapsulated the themes generated for the group of social workers, shown in Figure 6.2. This was created to present the findings in a way which would encourage the reader to understand the whole of the phenomenon comprised of different parts. In this way, the themes were not fragmented from the whole and therefore the nature of lived experience could be conveyed.

Gillian also provided a table which showed how each theme had been formed from the corresponding individual social workers' experiences. This was followed by a discussion of the group themes in turn, using examples and interpretative dialogue to explore, explain and justify. Figure 6.3 shows one example of the table for theme Navigating landscape and place in this example study.

In the left-hand column of the table the subordinate themes for the theme Navigating landscape and place are provided. Individual participants' experiences have been mapped to these in the right-hand columns so the pattern of how the themes were generated for the group are shown. A subsequent discussion of each theme was then included in the presentation, illustrated by examples and verbatim extracts from the social workers' individual accounts.

Figure 6.2 A visual web of group themes in IPA (Ferguson 2021: 141)

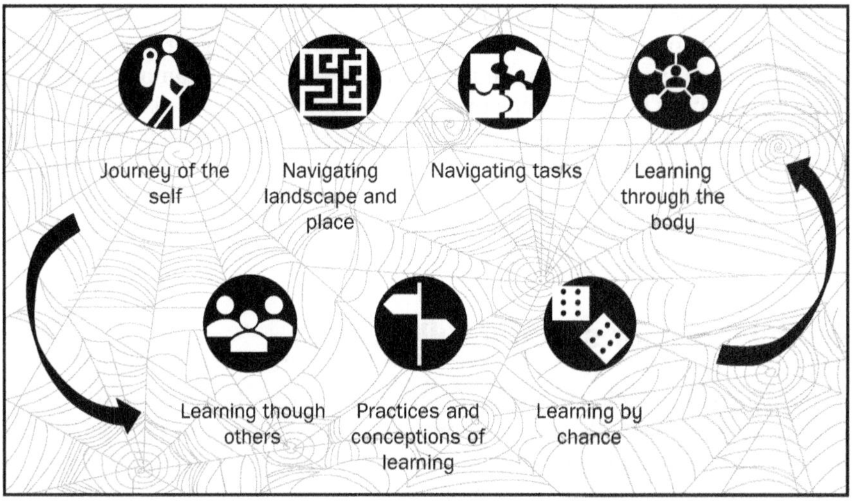

Figure 6.3 Image of group theme table developed from individual participant experiences (Ferguson 2021: 146)

	Boab	Carol	Reuben	Chloe	Kathleen	Sophie	Sylvia	Caroline	Maisie	Stuart	Jade	Karl	Makine	Danny
Navigating landscape and place	x	x	x	x	x	x	x	x	x	x	x	x	x	x
Diverse places		x	x	x	x	x		x	x	x				
Isolation	x							x	x	x	x		x	
No route map				x			x	x		x		x		
Different worlds			x					x		x			x	
Battle	x	x		x		x	x	x					x	
Aspects and elements	x		x	x	x					x	x	x	x	x

The examples from these studies show how commitment to the idiographic, phenomenological and interpretative elements of the research has been sustained in the presentation stage. They are all very different but highlight and give space to individual examples rooted in the data of lived experience and are set in context of the themes formed through the sense-making quest. All are from the representation of findings in doctoral theses, therefore there was scope to include a high level of detail and discussion. Within smaller-scale studies, journal articles, other publications or resources, the challenge of presenting IPA findings is even greater. It can be necessary to select one example or case to discuss in detail or focus on some examples of your findings to discuss depending on your audience or publication. In many IPA studies there is such rich detail that it would be possible to provide a detailed account of each theme and its relationship to the whole. Remember that with IPA studies, the reader joins the hermeneutic circle as a further sense-maker when they encounter your findings.

Reviewing your study – full circle

We introduced a holistic model to support the effective design of an IPA social work research project. We now encourage you to consider how your study can be reviewed by considering how the integrated elements have been used and where your findings sit in the knowledge landscape. Figure 6.4 shows the questions which can be used to review your study in relation to the integrated elements that we have worked through in the book.

You can explore each of the elements in turn, by considering how well this has worked for your study. It is also important to consider how everything has woven together in your research to enable you to generate rich data and make sense of this. What you have discovered is at the heart of the diagram, but the paths that have led you there have involved all the different components of your design and effective use of your chosen methods. If there are areas of your research that have not gone as planned, or where you have reflected that

Figure 6.4 A model for reviewing IPA social work research

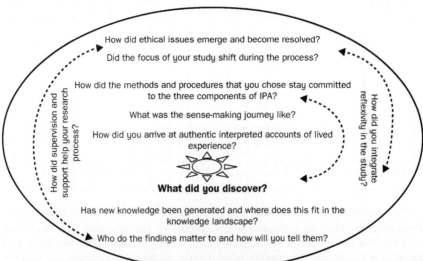

you would do very differently in the future, recognise these as limitations. It is important to reflect on the limitations honestly within any reports that you provide. Critically reflecting on your research provides an ethical audit that positions you well for defending the criticism and scrutiny of others. You will also be able to identify areas for further research by considering the limitations or scope of your study. You might have highlighted areas in your study that warrant further exploration, or new research questions. Having the skills to review your research will also continue to enhance your ability to critically engage with other studies, evaluating their design and findings.

Positioning your findings in the knowledge landscape

In Chapter 3 we explored the context of your study in relation to social work practice and policy and the available literature from previous research. You will have identified a gap in the literature and anticipated that your research could contribute to more understanding of your chosen topic. Now that your research is complete, think about how you can articulate any new ideas and insights that are supported by your data. How does the way that you have represented your findings help position or demonstrate the new knowledge that has been generated? There is usually a practice-related imperative in the focus of social work research and ethical drivers for undertaking a project. You might want to think about who the findings matter to or who these will be most relevant for. Thinking about the relationship of your findings to specific practice areas of social work is helpful. In many ways, you should consider how you can market the findings to those who are interested, or who you think should be interested in hearing about them. If you have confidence in the integrity and quality of your study, then sharing your findings can be exciting. Having designed your study with a clear, ethical framework and reviewed your approach, you can be confident in expressing what you have discovered.

Making a difference in social work

It is also important to think about what you want to achieve by sharing your findings. Impact is often talked about in academic arenas but can remain mysterious to many researchers. Essentially you are exploring the difference that your research has made to activities in the social work field. In a well-designed study you will have clearly identified potential beneficiaries of your research at an early stage; indeed this may be one of your central motivating factors for the whole project. Your research focus might have been very explicit in seeking to understand an issue or area of practice that could be changed. Alternatively, you might have studied the lived experiences of social workers as in the example studies. The centrality of people at the heart of social work practice is nonetheless key. In Sarah and Gillian's example studies, the lived experiences of people who were in receipt of social work services had a profound, career-long impact on their professional practice and personal lives. In the example study, Gillian had originally wanted to explore how to improve workplace learning for social workers. The focus was refined to take a step back to understand what the experience of this phenomenon was. In terms of making a difference beyond the study, the new insights ended up directly connecting to ways of thinking about improvement. The connections between social work as a profession and the fit with IPA, that have been explored in the early sections of this book, mean that your research findings are likely to be valued in the field particularly as they draw from lived experiences. Different scales of project are equally valuable in offering new ways to understand people's experiences and influence on social work practice.

Developing a clear plan for impact and showing the difference that has been made can maximise the learning from and influence of your research. Be confident to share your findings, however, as with all other stages of your project, having a plan will keep you on track. Reed (2018) identifies key principles, steps to achieve impact and details about the types of difference that research can make. Several important types of impact are likely with social work IPA studies: understanding and awareness; health and wellbeing; policy; cultural; and social. Thinking through the needs and priorities of those who would be interested in your research is framed as empathy in Reed's approach to impact (Reed 2018). Is there likely to be a reaction to your findings that heighten controversy? Consider what the likely questions or criticisms there might be from those who will be reading about the research. Reflecting on whether people will understand an issue or experience better than they did before, based on your research, is one way to consider this. Alternatively, does the research contribute to new or emerging policy or guidance for social work practice? Design when and how you communicate your findings, thinking about the best way to present the necessary detail. You might want to develop a clear briefing report or develop a strategy for dissemination on social media. You need to be aware of the context of your research, as outlined in Part 1 of this Book, to be able to maximise how you can use your findings to make a difference.

Summary points

- **Representation matters:** Have you selected a way to represent your findings effectively?
- **Lived experiences:** Do your findings stay true to interpreted accounts of lived experience?
- **Holistic review:** Use the trigger questions in the review model to evaluate your research project and identify limitations.
- **Contribution to knowledge:** Be clear on where the knowledge you have generated fits into the literature.

- **Generate impact:** Identify who the findings matter to, who needs to hear about your study and how you are going to tell them.

This chapter has explored the journey of your research project, including how this can be reviewed. Chapter 7 will now turn back to consider the essential role and process of supervision for IPA social work research. Although the chapter comes in after considering the research journey, and focuses primarily on doctoral supervision, it is vital to develop an effective supervisory alliance at the outset of any project. Our holistic model positions supervision as a crucial guiding component around a study. Chapter 7 considers use of supervision and support from the perspectives of both researcher and supervisor.

7 Supervising social work research through IPA

Chapter aims:

- to provide a brief overview of supervision of social work students and practitioners
- to discuss supervisory practice of research using IPA
- to outline a framework for supervision throughout the research process.

Introduction

Supervision of research, or being supervised when conducting research, requires an understanding of the methodological approach by both parties. However, little guidance exists as to what constitutes good supervisory practice when using IPA and anecdotal feedback from those being supervised is that often IPA is not fully understood. Anonymous comments by delegates at a recent conference illustrate such inconsistent experiences and suggest that this is an ongoing issue:

> I was having to teach my supervisor how to do IPA.

> It was like going through a jungle, I had no supervision nor guidance.

> I am privileged to have supervisors who understand IPA as I know so many do not.

The aim of this chapter then is to provide an overview of good supervisory practice in IPA, whether in its provision or its receipt, and to suggest a framework for both supervisor and researcher. The framework we offer covers the process from the design through to the doing and at its defence. Throughout, we explore how influential the supervisory process is and acknowledge the difference, if any, between what we are terming 'formal supervision' required of academic institutions and 'less formal supervision' as may be needed through, for example, a workplace study. We also briefly consider the impact of supervision of an individual, peer supervision and of a group. As has been the case previously in this book, this chapter draws on the doctoral experiences of its authors, one of whom had supervisors who were both qualified social workers and understood IPA as a methodological approach, whilst the second had supervisors who were not social workers and did not know IPA. Both authors have experience in supervising doctoral students using IPA methodology. It also draws from their knowledge of convening a doctoral studies programme.

Supervision and social work

Arguably, supervision of social work practice – whether of a student or qualified practitioner – is a complex task but one which ultimately sets out to promote the best outcome for the person in receipt of services. There exists a wealth of advice on the supervision of social work students and qualified practitioners. In relation to both, the literature summarises four distinct yet interdependent functions (Morrison 2001, 2005):

- management – ensuring competent/accountable practice and performance
- development – facilitating continuous professional development
- support – providing personal and emotional support to workers
- mediation – engaging the individual with the organisation.

Except for mediation, another commentator echoes these aspects (Tsui 2005) and describes supervision as related functions whereby first the administrative typically has tasks that are associated with 'getting the job done', including work planning, monitoring and reviewing. Next, the educational function sets out to develop knowledge, skills and values and, last, the supportive function provides both psychological and interpersonal assistance. This third function is said to be of particular importance when working in an emotive area of practice. The emotional impact of social work and the need for supervision because of this impact is well documented (Kadushin and Harkness 2002; Ingram 2013; Kettle et al. 2016; McGarvey-Gill 2023). Moreover, the argument that supervision should provide a reflective space is also well rehearsed. For example, Earle et al. (2017: 3) remind us that, 'reflective supervision offers a safe space for a practitioner to slow down and think, explore possibilities, look for meaning and a way to do their work well'. However, as Ruch argues, there is also no simple formula to reflective supervision (Ruch 2013 in Earle et al. 2017). She instead offers pointers: that it is driven by the experience of the learner; that it provides space and context for the learning; that the supervisor takes the role of the facilitator, thereby enabling the learner to own decisions; and last, that it is seen as part of an ongoing learning process (Ruch 2013 in Earle et al. 2017). Nonetheless, the quality of supervision of social work practice varies, regardless of its function and of the guidance available, and this is also the case in relation to doctoral and other research supervision which itself has a related purpose.

Supervision and academic work

Supervision, or the person(s) acting as supervisor, is the terminology used in most universities in the UK for academics who have responsibility for overseeing the progress of individual students' research studies. Ideally the supervisor should have knowledge of the subject area being researched, along with a mature understanding of research processes, including a range of methodological approaches. Moreover, supervisor(s) should have knowledge of the institutional rules and regulations concerning doctoral study, a tension which this chapter will also suggest needs to be considered through the lens of supervision.

Much guidance exists for supervision of doctoral students, not least the processes and guidelines that exist in each academic institution where doctoral study is taking place. Supervision is provided so that the student who is learning to become an independent researcher does so with appropriate skills, value base and knowledge of research processes. To enable this, most supervisors are required to engage in in-depth conversations with their student about their research and to guide them through the research process, including methodological options available to best fit the aim of the research.

However, whilst research can take place as part of a formal educational process, and this is the focus of this chapter, it may not always take place in a university. It can be less formal, such as carrying out smaller projects – for example, in the workplace. In such instances, supervisors may be in a mentor role or have line management responsibility either for you as a researcher and/or accountability for the research and it is here that boundaries may blur. In all cases, access to appropriate supervision is beneficial and this should involve the agreeing of expectations on the part of supervisor and supervisee.

Using the general practice of social work and academic supervisory practices as a backdrop, we now go on to examine doctoral supervision in IPA. We will do so through three stages: the design, the doing and the defence.

The design

Most doctoral research design follows a conventional format. For research using IPA as its methodological approach in social work, we will in this chapter refer to the framework first introduced in Chapter 3, which situates supervision as encompassing the process and integral to it. We will now explore the design according to aim, literature search and review, sample, data collection and analysis.

Aim

As with all research design, to begin, the research aim or objective must be decided and is then usually presented in the form of a question according to the interest in the phenomenon being studied. The supervisory process sets out to help the researcher to hone their question (or aim) and, in turn, to discuss whether IPA or another methodological approach is the correct one given this. Examples of such questions according to different methodological approaches have been provided in Chapter 3. For IPA, it is important for the supervisor to explore with the supervisee how the research is committed to its components: phenomenology, idiography and hermeneutics. What appears to be a simple task can, however, take several iterations and is usually underpinned by a literature search and review undertaken to identify the current knowledge of the phenomenon and identify gaps in it. The role of supervision at this stage is therefore a guiding one, the purpose of which is to both empathise and question. For Sarah, supervision afforded an opportunity to interrogate the focus of her research intention and concerned a dialogue about the concept of experience and identity. Sarah was setting out to explore role fulfilment of a particular legal social work role. To do so, it was pivotal to tease out the possible overlap between role, task and function as part of identity and in turn to understand what was meant by experience. The notion that Sarah's research was to explore the in-depth experience of undertaking a particular aspect of a legal role, from the perspective of a homogenous group of practitioners by a researcher who had also undertaken that same work, meant that Sarah's research was a good fit with IPA. For Gillian, supervision provided helpful interrogation of the study focus, which was refined from broad, multiple interests to a clear, definite research question. Having been intent on using Action Research, supervisors also skilfully guided Gillian to explore phenomenology and best fit with her fundamental quest.

Literature search and review

Understanding the current literature in relation to the proposed study is a given in all research and usually happens before any data are collected. Supervision of this process therefore follows a usual pattern. Any student must demonstrate an ability to undertake a search of the literature and undertake a critical analysis of that which exists to situate their own proposed topic within what is found. For studies using IPA such a process is usual and the role of supervision should advise on this process. It is nonetheless helpful for the supervisory process to include a reminder about how any evidence gleaned at this stage will need, as with the researcher's own anecdotal and professional knowledge, to be set to one side during analysis. Such bracketing is fundamental to research using IPA.

Sample

Often, in research that adopts a qualitative methodological approach such as IPA, debate ensues in the shadow of positivism as to the 'correct' sample size. Such tensions are fundamental to research using IPA as it is usually the case that less is more. In our experience, the role of supervision in relation to sample size is to discuss with the doctoral candidate the intention of the research and in turn to agree what an appropriate sample size might be. As we have discussed in Chapter 3, the aim is to achieve an in-depth exploration of the meaning -making of the participant and in turn the sense-making the researcher makes of this. This double hermeneutic takes time and it is likely that, the bigger the sample, not only is there a possibility that homogeneity may be lost but so too the depth of the meaning-making and understanding. For us then the role of supervision it is to provide confidence to the candidate that a homogenous sample is key, small sample size notwithstanding.

Data collection

Data collection in IPA studies is undertaken through an increasingly wide range of methods. To date, the most used is the semi-structured interview. For IPA researchers who are also social workers, supervision is key when understanding the differences and similarities between an interview that is done for social work purposes and one for the purposes of research. As was seen in Chapter 2, whilst there may be some overlap between social work and qualitative social work research, an interview for a research study is to elicit data for a different purpose. Supervision therefore is to guide the candidate through any potential differences and to deal with any ethical issues that might arise. For instance, in Sarah's research if there had been a disclosure of unlawful practice then the interview would have needed to stop, and advice sought from her supervisory team as to next steps. These steps would be guided by Sarah's own Code of Conduct by which she abides as a registered social worker. This was a similar process for Gillian, where supervisors stressed the importance of considering how things would be managed, supporting an effective professional discussion about hypothetical scenarios. Attention to ethical issues remained a feature of supervision throughout the process.

Other data collection methods include focus groups, the completion of diaries and, in Sarah's case, participant-drawn pictures and the discussion thereof. Whatever the method, supervision as with all research is to guide the candidate and advise.

Analysis

According to Smith and colleagues, one of the main roles of supervising in IPA involves fostering a sense of manageability in the analytic process (Smith et al. 2022: 77). We agree. As first discussed in Chapter 4, for Sarah the manageability came about because of the suggestion by her supervisory team to consider the use of a computer software data management tool. Taking time to become familiar with the package and the learning thereafter required consistent advice from her supervisory team as well as the permission to move away from the empirical process whilst doing so. Ultimately this 'break' had a positive impact. Having taken the decision to use such a package to manage the data, Sarah took time to understand how to use the tool according to the methodological approach, in this instance IPA. To assist, Sarah stepped back from the data and spent time learning the functions of the package but crucially how best this might fit according to IPA. To that end the textbook by Bazelely and

Jackson (2013) provided a solid grounding which Sarah used to adapt to IPA, a process which she went on to discuss in detail in a journal article (Vicary et al. 2017). In brief, the use of this tool enabled the analysis process to be contained: all data was imported into the package and in turn analysis was undertaken through the creation of links and memos, each of which provided an audit trail to show quality and validity. Through pictorial representation of the way in which this was done by screen shots in that same article (Vicary et al. 2017), Sarah was also able to show the double hermeneutic in action. Moreover, Sarah was able to export reports either of the data and links to them and/or of the reflective journal and send these to her supervisors in advance of supervision. This afforded an opportunity for in-depth discussion and an opportunity to check interpretation. As Smith and colleagues contend, the use of supervision helps develop the coherence and plausibility of the interpretation (Smith et al. 2022: 75) a point repeated by Smith and Nizza (2022: 32) who suggest that to share data with supervisors (using analysis packages/write up of codes/themes/groups of themes) – especially for a new researcher – may be that of independent audit. For Gillian, one of the most important aspects of supervision was being able to discuss the messiness of the process and seek reassurance on the direction of the study. Supervisors have a clear role to balance the exploration of what is happening for the researcher and provide guidance whilst also promoting autonomous choices.

Having discussed the role of supervision in the design of the research, we will now go on to explore the part supervision plays during the undertaking of it: the doing. We do so through interviewing and ethical considerations.

The doing

Interviewing

As suggested earlier in this book, the fit between IPA and social work is a good one – not least regarding the skill involved in undertaking an interview which is both empathic and questioning, the two hermeneutic strands of IPA. For Smith and colleagues, 'interviewing is a skill …which develops best when supported by supervisory, peer and participant feedback' (Smith et al. 2022: 54). We suggest that people who are social workers and undertake research already have a skilled aptitude in interviewing because of the nature of their profession. The role of supervision is one of enabling the social worker to understand their role as a researcher as opposed to a social worker. We therefore suggest that any supervisor of an IPA research project in social work revisits the debate in Chapter 2. Supervision will need to consider how a social work researcher differentiates between IPA as a research approach and their 'day job' and also that this will involve the learning and unlearning of skills to apply them in a different context. It is also suggested that a supervisor helps review any interview guide (Smith and Nizza 2022: 22). Other more practical matters, albeit with this different role in mind, are to review any pilot or practice work such as interviews. This may be to help a researcher if they are not used to interviewing or, as may be the case with social work, that they are used to interviewing but for a different reason.

In short, the role of supervisor in IPA and social work research might then be to have an objective eye as to the conduct of the interview and whether it is being conducted for research reasons or has a social work slant, or even if this difference matters. For Sarah, who was a long-standing social worker steeped in the process which she was intending to research, supervision helped to negotiate the unlearning and learning of her skills safely.

Ethical considerations

Dealing with emotive topics and looking after the self is always a consideration when exploring people's lived experience and the meaning they make of it. Supervision should include space to check this out and to ensure that any candidate is aware of protocols and has a support strategy. Similarly, research participants and their needs relating to potential distress must be considered. As in all research projects, the supervisor is usually the first point of contact. Other strategies, such as providing contact detail of support agencies and follow up, are as important. The practicalities of obtaining ethics approval for IPA studies require the same attention as for all research. The role of supervision is again to guide the candidate through this process.

Our experiences in supervising doctoral candidates who are considering the use of IPA as their research approach is that, at all stages, it is useful for the supervisor to return to the integrated model of IPA for social work research as was introduced in Chapter 3. This can help review where and how the study is aligned with the necessary phenomenological, idiographic and hermeneutic requirements. Often researchers will focus on the first two of these components, while the hermeneutic aspect is less clear in the designing and doing. It will be vital in the defence that all three are clear, and it is to this that we now turn.

The defence

Defence of a thesis, literally a viva voce, is a formal academic process in which a candidate justifies their work from aim through to findings, including limitations. An integral role of supervision concerns this defence, and for IPA this means an ongoing questioning of the candidate as to the methodological approach. Supervision should always have in mind whether what is being undertaken at any stage is IPA. For example, should a candidate suggest first at the analysis stage that they are to analyse using the stages suggested by Smith and colleagues then it is likely that IPA has not been the underpinning approach throughout, either in terms of its underpinning theoretical stance or commitment to the sense-making, of the participant or the analyst. IPA is an in-depth approach at all stages and is especially highlighted as such during analysis, which cannot be rushed. Supervision must be aware of and support this time taking. A parallel process therefore is to prepare the candidate for their defence in the round as well as through the stages. These stages will involve specific decisions taken concerning sample size, homogeneity, validity and rigour, including how an audit trail is established to warrant any findings. Limitations should also be acknowledged. We argue that there may be a tension between undertaking 'true' IPA and having to abide by academic conventions, one of which is defending your work. It is important to be aware of this possible tension and be especially so given the ways in which different institutions may require write ups of doctoral theses. Using the framework for reviewing an IPA study, provided in Chapter 6, can help strengthen confidence and articulation of how the study has been undertaken.

Other types of supervision

Whilst this chapter has mostly focused upon the relationship between you as an individual doctoral candidate and your supervisor(s) or supervisory team, other research can be conducted in different contexts, whether that is for a project in a service in which you work or as part of a funded research study. We introduced such networks and communities of support in Chapter 3. In all cases establishing expectations is key. The relationship between your responsibility as the interpreter and the input of your supervisor, however named, is pivotal to research and this is no different for any research that uses IPA. The relationship becomes more complicated if you are undertaking research as a group. Ultimately, you hold responsibility for your research, and part of this is recognising the roles of key figures and of organisations and arguably establishing your independence of them through justification of what you have done and why.

Conclusion

For those new to IPA as a methodological approach, supervision is instrumental. However, as the anecdotes that opened this chapter suggest, the quality of such supervision is inconsistent. It has been our aim in this chapter to provide a guide, with examples, to address this inconsistency. For social work research using IPA, whilst it is not the case that supervisors have to be social workers per se, an understanding of social work as a profession and indeed the role of supervision within that is an important facet. Social workers, for example, are used to undertaking interviews, but interviewing for a research purpose requires an understanding of the difference of purpose and outcome, a discussion which was addressed in Chapter 2.

Summary points

- It is important to think about how supervision is planned to hold the research process.
- Supervisors and supervisees need to understand IPA and that it is a whole approach.
- The model for IPA social work research can help guide the process regardless of the purpose.

Social work ethics, values and skills can support effective data collection, management and analysis throughout the study to generate authentic interpreted accounts of lived experience, and this interface is one we have suggested throughout this book. Supervision of the study is therefore as important. We also hope that for those being supervised using IPA for the first time from whatever discipline, this chapter provides guidance as to the expectation you should have in delivery. Likewise, we trust this helps those who are supervising research using IPA for the first time. We now move to Part 3 of the book, to look to the horizon of IPA in social work.

Part 3

Determining Social Work Knowledge Using IPA

8 | IPA in social work: the present and future

Chapter aims:

- to review the current use of IPA in social work
- to summarise findings including any significant trends and implications
- to look to the horizon of future directions for IPA in social work.

Introduction

This chapter sets out to explore the current use of IPA as an approach in social work summarised through the authors' understanding. First, we summarise social work using IPA through chronology and content. We then comment upon perceptions in relation to sample size and use of the approach. Then, we comment on the development of the approach for social work and its future horizons as we perceive them.

Turning to chronology, it is perhaps not surprising to note, given the date of the publication of the first edition of the IPA textbook (Smith et al. 2009), that the first literature reporting the use of IPA as a methodological approach for social work knowledge appeared in the early 2010s. Publications thereafter are steady. Whilst not high in number, the growth does tend to indicate an increased awareness of IPA as an approach in social work, including its use to provide knowledge for the profession and explorations of how the approach could fit. Our experiences as doctoral research supervisors have also led us to notice that IPA is being widely used in social work and other studies as the preferred methodology for exploring lived experience. We believe that it is imperative that as studies develop, the elements of IPA are fully integrated in the research design. Emerging studies and subsequent publications are therefore anticipated, contributing to the body of literature in the IPA social work field. We also anticipate more debate surrounding the fit of this as an approach for social work research.

The approach

There are matters concerning perceptions of the approach in social work that are of interest which primarily concern perceived limitations. It is pleasing to note where the sample size is reported these on the whole indicate small numbers. However, where authors discuss the limitation of their work often the small sample size was viewed as such with statements such as this would not be generalisable, nor would it be representative of the population. To us, this misses the idiographic nature of IPA research and suggests a possible and unwarranted lack of confidence in the validity of the findings.

We also note that some literature appears to view IPA literally as analysis, using the framework identified by Smith et al. (2009). Smith himself refers to the provision of this framework as a way of helping those new to the approach to break analysis up into manageable chunks but also points out the importance of the interpretative work of the analyst at each stage (Smith 2011a: 58). To only use the framework then perhaps suggests a weak understanding of IPA as a methodological approach and suggests a mechanistic understanding of IPA. What is encouraging is that other literature reports an understanding as more holistic, referring not only to the underpinning theoretical influences but of using it to capture the essence of authentic understanding and giving voice to a significant experience. Some other misunderstandings pertain. For instance, the role of the interpreter is viewed as bias, perhaps not fully understanding the central role of interpretation to IPA.

Regarding the development of IPA for social work, which aligns well with the focus of this chapter and our underpinning reason for this book, one debate revolves around a combination of approaches. One critique of IPA is that it has psychological depth but lacks social context (Houston and Mullen-Jensen 2011) and such a combination may serve to address this. Indeed, these authors did themselves originally put forward a combination of the use of Social Domains Theory to help situate any research in the social context (Houston and Mullan-Jensen 2011). A second suggestion is that to combine approaches would further enable the co-constitutive nature of the 'double hermeneutic' in which practitioners are engaged and that this combination is particularly suited for qualitative research in social work (Hood 2016: 171). Such methodological advances will undoubtedly be a future direction. Combining IPA with a particular method, in this instance visual, is also a possible development (Bartoli 2020 and Vicary 2021). For Bartoli, asking participants to talk about objects meaningful to the phenomenon for them helped facilitate the different accounts adding another dimension which fits well with the flexibility of IPA. Vicary used participant-drawn images which are used to illustrate her 'pearl' (Smith et al. 2011c) which she interpreted from one participant. Vicary suggests that to ask participants to draw a picture of their lived experience of the phenomenon in question helps elicit thoughts and feelings which might not otherwise emerge, especially in a profession which is word based ordinarily. We have noticed use of photographs, rich pictures and other creative methods being increasingly used to trigger discussion and tap into lived experience in studies that we have seen.

Overall IPA is viewed as an approach that aligns well with social work in seeking to place the person and their lived experience at the centre. This approach underpins this book and there is a strong theme in the literature that IPA is value-driven and upholds respect for the dignity, expertise and viewpoint of others allied to a close regard for potential sources of inequality and oppression in social relationships (Hood 2016: 171). Other possible developments of the approach concern processes. These include learning about appropriate application of it along with ways of enabling quality and validity through reflection *inside* a computer software package (and discussed in more detail in Chapter 5).

Focus on identity

It is reported that research involving IPA has a strong focus on identity (Smith 2004). An overview of the use of IPA in social work would echo this. Up to this point the synergy between IPA and social work research has been explored through the lens of social work research undertaken to be of benefit to those in receipt of social work services. To that end, we have hinted that IPA is a good fit due to less intrusion and in turn a greater possibility of avoiding ethical pitfalls. However, social work research can also concern that evidence which is gathered to bolster the actual profession itself. Arguably, the latter also means that the former will benefit, but the subtle difference is worthy of consideration when exploring context in this way. Meaning and context are said to be inextricably linked in qualitative research, a connection that is also possible when using IPA as a methodology. In this book we suggest context in relation to the participant, be they the individual with lived experience in receipt of services or individuals with lived experience of undertaking this delivery. Smith's view is that while IPA focuses, first and foremost, on the individual and experiential context, other studies will also include a more explicit social context and the experience will be framed with a discussion of social and political forces which will be tackled in different ways (Smith 2011b). It is to this social context that we now turn.

Critique

As has been noted, one critique of IPA from a social work perspective is its psychological depth and that this may detract from other considerations. It is therefore suggested that there is a need for its application to widen to allow consideration of socio-cultural situated-ness, thereby also allowing a strengthening of the quality of IPA (Todorova 2011). Smith's response to this argument is to defend the continuing focus which IPA must have on individual experience, but he also concedes that in future an explicit social context would provide a more rounded synthesis (Smith 2011b). Such epistemological adaptability has been discussed in the literature, is welcomed as a healthy situation and is accepted as a way in which IPA could develop (Larkin et al. 2006: 117). It is our view that social work research using IPA will help to do so.

Others agree that the epistemological basis of IPA should change, or as described in its title it should have width as well as depth (Houston and Mullan-Jensen 2011). This opinion is of relevance to this book since it is made in relation to the use of IPA as a research methodology for social work, the practice of which Houston and Mullan-Jensen contend also attempts to understand meaning in the context of wider social processes. They suggest that if IPA is to be used as a qualitative research methodology in social work, it also needs to enable this breadth of understanding and its meaning (Houston and Mullan-Jensen, 2011). For them, this alignment will permit the qualitative social work researcher to understand both the psychological and sociological dimensions of existence (Houston and Mullan-Jensen 2011: 266). Todorova meanwhile contends that as researchers identify limiting or stigmatising social meanings, a constructionist epistemology will more clearly explicate and question them (Todorova 2011: 36).

One limitation of our approach in this chapter concerns its brevity. Also, we have only discussed the use of IPA in social work in the UK. Literature published in wider geographical settings may tell of its geographical influence. Moreover, our knowledge is not fulsome. For example, a very quick search of the *British Journal of Learning Disabilities* produced 27 articles that cited IPA as the methodological approach, most of which concerned the lived experience of adults and their networks. It would be interesting to understand why IPA seemingly lends itself to knowledge making in this field. It is something that Smith himself wondered when discussing developing the methodology to reach different populations (Smith 2011).

The future

Echoing Smith's own thoughts as to the future of IPA, four targets are recommended (Smith 2011: 25): first, an examination of a body of work that already exists within the discipline with any new research being discussed in relation to this extant work. From our knowledge, it is probably the case that such a body for social work does not yet exist. However, the trend is growing, and such a target may well be possible in the future. Second, Smith suggests that its use is taken up in cognate disciplines. It is our belief that IPA is a good fit with social work, and we have written this book with that target in mind. Third, Smith makes a plea for integration between the quantitative and qualitative in psychology, an argument which is not unique to that discipline and from our perspective is one with which we would not disagree for social work. Last, Smith would like IPA to fill the gap in the literature which explores prevention, health promotion and, in turn, the working together of quantitative and qualitive research to help understand and change behaviour. This target is an interesting one for social work which would shy away from the provision of such prescriptive knowledge. It is our view that the strength of IPA is its alignment with the value base of social work in that it seeks to place the person at the centre and to explore what a significant experience means for them at its core.

Summary points

- The use of IPA has a small but growing corpus in the UK.
- Some misunderstandings are found – not least that IPA is a framework of analysis.
- There is evidence that IPA is becoming known in social work more holistically.
- Future directions could include increased use and developments in the approach for social work.

This chapter has sought to explore the current and future direction of IPA in social work and as such ends Part 3 of this book. The Conclusion that follows will bring together the book's major themes.

Conclusion

The complexities of social work roles and tasks can be hard to articulate, coupled with the fact that social work takes place within diverse settings and multi-disciplinary contexts. We suggest that the potential of IPA for generating professional social work knowledge is enormous, and it is this belief that is the underlying premise of this book. This conclusion provides a summary of key points stemming from the ideas that have been explored.

At the outset, our foundation chapter describes the inception of IPA as a research methodology, situating it within the qualitative research paradigm. The description includes IPA's theoretical underpinnings and an examination of the lived experience and its relevance for social work. The suggestion that IPA seeks to understand, give voice and make meaning of a phenomenon or person in context chimes with the underlying premise of social work, a profession which to paraphrase van Manen (2016) works with discretion, intuition and tact. These abstract notions for us are best explored through IPA which attempts to uncover the nature and meaning of the reality of people's experiences in the world, or to be more precise, the social world. In both IPA and social work there is a central role of analysis and interpretation which run in parallel.

Our aim in the second chapter then is to position IPA and social work as a good fit. We do so by providing a background to social work and social work research and by discussing other methodologies hitherto popular for social work by way of a comparison. Through a discussion of the synergies between social work and IPA we argue that the dynamics of research in social work more readily fits with IPA. It is a good methodological fit since it explores experience and specifically the sense made of it from the viewpoint of an individual or homogenous group. The role of the researcher is fundamental. We do, however, sound a note of caution, as subtle nuances exist between social work and social work research, including IPA, and these must be considered. Such ethical challenges pertain to all research and are particularly sensitive when exploring personal experience where there may also be a need for intervention. We are grateful to the reviewers of our proposal who suggested the inclusion of supervision. Overseeing these nuances are, we believe, a particular need for social work and IPA.

To underpin our conviction that IPA is a good fit, we turn in Chapter 3 to consider the details involved in setting up an effective IPA social work research study. The holistic model introduced here for us draws together the key ingredients of IPA social work research. It talks directly to you as a researcher and uses our own experiences as doctoral researchers which we trust brings helpful insight into the process for novices and will also help guide those with greater experience. Messages about the connection between the intention of a study and the intricacies of the research process are sum-marised. The model is also provided as a visual aide-memoir so that the processes of undertaking such a study are contained but also reinforced. As we found in our overview of the current state of research in social work using IPA, some researchers use the analysis part only. IPA is a whole approach and should be treated as such.

The second part of the book has been designed to follow the research jour-ney in traditional chronological format for formal academic studies. To begin, Chapter 4 reinforces the process of designing IPA social work research. Again, we provide examples from the authors to illustrate. Our intention is to show that even though no two research studies are the same they should, from an IPA perspective, be based upon and constantly refer to the same holistic premise. Our purpose in writing this book is to reinforce the message not just that IPA is a good fit with social work but that when undertaking studies using IPA the whole approach must be followed. As for the detail, we strongly urge reflection on how you are crafting the design of your research throughout so that you retain the commitment to IPA. Suggestions are provided to help you undertake this process, all of which will also be of help in supervision. Chapters 5 and 6 continue this journey, with the former exploring aspects of analysis that arrive at interpreted accounts of lived experience and the latter turning to what is arguably the real purpose of any research, which is how best to disseminate so that it makes a difference in people's lives.

Chapter 7 concludes Part 2 and is in response to our reviewers who very helpfully suggested that including a focus on supervision would make the book more rounded. We agree. In this chapter we set out to address what is a gap in the current advice for both those in receipt of supervision and those providing it. To do so we situate supervision for IPA in the formal academic context whilst acknowledging that research does take place in other settings. The expecta-tions we suggest are transferrable.

Having delved into the detail of social work and IPA in Part 2, we wanted in the final part to stand back and have a wider oversight of IPA and social work. So Chapter 8 concludes the book with an examination of the current state of social work and IPA in the UK. While not based on a systematic review, our knowledge gave rise to several matters which resonate with our reason for providing this book and which suggest possible future directions. Post-intentional phenomenology (Vagle 2018) integrates the social construc-tion of a phenomenon, and the influence of culture and social class can help explain and interpret. This speaks to the discussion around context that we have referred to in Part 1 and Part 3 of the book. Shifts and creativities across phenomenological approaches are exciting for our future shared learning. The body of published social work research using IPA is small but growing. We are also aware as supervisors and convenors of social work doctorates and doctoral programmes that interest is also rising. Our findings were some-what bittersweet. On the one hand, it is clear from the way in which some studies are reported that IPA is not followed holistically. On the other hand, there is also some fine-grained understanding of it as a research approach and some increasing debate of the fit with social work. We believe that statements to the effect that the relative dearth of studies is surprising should become a thing of the past. To that end, we feel vindicated in the rationale for writing this book. It has been a personal journey for both of us and for the most part an enjoyable one. We trust that it helps raise awareness of social work and IPA and provides enthusiasm for its application.

Appendix: Further reading and resources for IPA social work research

Here we recommend a few of our favourite reading and resources on, and related to, IPA social work research. We just introduce and briefly explain why we like them.

***Interpretative Phenomenological Analysis*, 2nd edn.** (2022) Jonathan
  Smith, Paul Flowers and Michael Larkin, London: Sage.
Everyone engaging in IPA can learn at first-hand from the authors of the first and second editions of this volume which introduces, underpins and explores the approach. An easily digestible resource for the novice and experienced researcher alike.

***Researching Lived Experience: Human Science for an Action Sensitive
  Pedagogy*, 2nd edn.** (2015) Max van Manen, Oxford: Routledge.
A marvellous book which helps the reader get to grips with researching the experience of the lifeworld. There is a focus on understanding the structure of the lifeworld and a discussion on the concept of human science which has immediate appeal to social work. The role of the researcher is given due attention, and this may particularly appeal to educational researchers.

***Crafting Phenomenological Research*, 2nd edn.** (2018) Mark D. Vagle,
  New York: Routledge.
An amazing resource which considers the in-depth process of phenomenological research and introduces the concept of post-intentional phenomenology. There is a clear appreciation of the importance of the intrapersonal research process in phenomenology. The book provides a solid philosophical foundation and accessible snapshots of the nuances within phenomenological research. Practical ideas and resources are hugely welcome throughout the book for those who are new to the subject but also those revisiting phenomenological research.

***Embodied Enquiry: Phenomenological Touchstones for Research.
  Psychotherapy and Spirituality*.** (2007) Les Todres, London: Palgrave
  Macmillan.
Les Todres' book is a wonderful read for those who are interested in the embodied nature of phenomenology. This book speaks to the phenomenological data but also the researcher's process. Unsurprisingly given the psychotherapy focus, this book appeals to those interested in in-depth therapeutic practice.

Todres explores the lived body as a way of both knowing and being in the world.

***Reflective Lifeworld Research*, 2nd edn.** (2008) Karin Dahlberg, Helena Dahlberg and Maria Nyström, Lund: Studentlitteratur.
A lovely volume that helps the researcher really tune into what we mean by lifeworld research. A focus on human experience and meaning is woven through this book which will appeal to those who wish to explore the philosophy alongside the practical approach to lifeworld research.

Doing Qualitative Research in Social Work. (2014) Ian Shaw and Sally Holland, London: Sage.
A comprehensive book for qualitative research connected to the social work context. Drawn from the authors' extensive academic and practice experience in social work, the content is detailed and authentic. Alongside clear information that contextualises social work research, there is a focus on methods and procedures. The concern of social work and associated research with social justice is an important inclusion.

***Doing Research in the Real World*, 3rd edn.** (2014) David Gray, London: Sage.
A favourite for researchers undertaking studies in their workplace or fields of practice. Gray's book and accompanying resources provide an easy-to-use guide. It is a comprehensive guide to get new researchers started that includes hints and tips for the insider-researcher.

Doing Work-Based Research: Approaches to Enquiry for Insider-Researchers. (2013) Carol Costley, Geoffrey Elliott and Paul Gibbs, London: Sage.
Another favourite from those who are engaged in real-world research in the places that they practise. This book is a great resource for considering the specific ethical issues for insider-researchers and connections with professional practice.

***Qualitative Data Analysis with NVIVO*, 2nd edn.** (2013) P. Bazeley and K. Jackson, London: Sage.
For those who are considering using a computer-aided software management tool to manage data, this book is a great resource to help you think about using your methodological approach with the tool in mind.

Birbeck University IPA portal

Birbeck University IPA webspace provides a hub of information, contacts and links to a widely used discussion forum on the research methodology. This remains a rich source for IPA researchers from any perspective. You can find the information online at http://www.ipa.bbk.ac.uk

Open University Social Work IPA network

The OU SWIPA network is a community of practice open to anyone interested in furthering use and knowledge of IPA for social work research. The network hosts annual seminars and other events to share learning from IPA social work research. For more information, please contact us at The Open University: swiparesearch@open.ac.uk

References

Anzul, M., Ely, M., Freidman, T. et al. (1991) *Doing Qualitative Research: Circles Within Circles*. London: Taylor and Francis.

Bartoli, A. (2020) Every picture tells a story: Combining interpretative phenomenological analysis with visual research, *Qualitative Social Work*, 19(5):1007–21.

Bazeley, P. and Jackson, K. (2013) *Qualitative Data Analysis with NVIVO*, 2nd edn. London: Sage.

Bevan, M.T. (2014) A method of phenomenological interviewing, *Qualitative Health Research*, 24(1): 136–44.

Charmaz, K. (2008) *Constructing Grounded Theory (Introducing Qualitative Methods series)* 2nd edn. London: Sage.

Checkland, P. (1980) *Systems Thinking, Systems Practice*. London: Wiley.

Chenail, R.J. (1995) Presenting qualitative data, *The Qualitative Report*, 2(3): 1–9. Available at https://nsuworks.nova.edu/tqr/vol2/iss3/5/ (accessed 26 May 2023).

Costley, C., Elliott, G. and Gibbs, P. (2013) *Doing Work Based Research: Approaches to Enquiry for Insider-Researchers*. London: Sage.

Dahlberg, K., Dahlberg, H. and Nystrom, M. (2008) *Reflective Lifeworld Research*. Lund: Studentlitteratur.

Earle, F., Fox, J., Webb, C. and Bowyer, S. with Flood, S. (ed.) (2017) *Reflective Supervision: An online resource pack*, Dartington, Devon: Research in Practice. Available at https://www.researchinpractice.org.uk/children/publications/2017/april/reflective-supervision-resource-pack-2017/ (accessed 21 September 2023).

Ferguson, G.M. (2021) 'When David Bowie created Ziggy Stardust' The Lived Experiences of Social Workers Learning Through Work. EdD thesis, Milton Keynes, The Open University. Available at https://oro.open.ac.uk/77930/ (accessed 26 May 2023)

Finlay, L. (2008) A dance between the reduction and the reflexivity: Explicating the phenomenological psychological attitude, *Journal of Phenomenological Psychology*, 39(1):1–32.

Finlay, L. (2011) *Phenomenology for Therapists: Researching the Lived World*. Chichester: Wiley-Blackwell.

Fongkaew, W. and Nilvarangkul, K. (2018) Editorial: Special issues and implications in action research, *Pacific Rim International Journal of Nursing Research*, 22(3): 175–77.

Garfinkel, H. (1967) *Studies in Ethnomethodology*. New York: Prentice-Hall.

Gil-Rodriguez, E. and Hefferon, K. (2012) Introduction to IPA Two Day Workshop Resource Pack (December). London: IPA Training.

Gilgun, J. (1994) Hand into glove. The grounded theory approach and social work practice research, in E. Sherman and W.J. Reid (eds) *Qualitative Research in Social Work*, pp. 115–25. New York: Columbia University Press.

Giorgi, A. (2010) Phenomenology and the practice of science, *Existential Analysis*, 21(1): 3–22.

Glaser, B.G. (1992) *Basics of Grounded Theory Analysis: Emergence Versus Forcing*. Mill Valley, CA: Sociology Press.

Glaser, B.G. and Strauss, A.L. (1967) *The Discovery of Grounded Theory: Strategies for Qualitative Research*. Mill Valley, CA: Sociology Press.

Gray, D. (2014) *Doing Research in the Real World*, 3rd edn. London: Sage.

Guillemin, M. (2004) Understanding illness: Using drawings as a research method, *Qualitative Health Research*, 14(2): 272–89.

Heidegger, M. (1962) *Being and Time*. Oxford: Blackwell.

Hood, R. (2016) Combining phenomenological and critical methodologies in qualitative research, *Qualitative Social Work*, 15(2):160–74.

Houston, S. and Mullan-Jensen, C. (2011) Towards depth and width in Qualitative Social Work: Aligning interpretative phenomenological analysis with the theory of social domains, *Qualitative Social Work*, 11(3): 266–81.

Hus, E. (2012) What we see and what we say: combining visual and verbal information within social work research, *British Journal of Social Work*, 42(8): 1440–59.

Ingram, R. (2013) Locating emotional intelligence at the heart of social work practice, *British Journal of Social Work*, 43(5): 987–1004.

Kadushin, A. and Harkness, D. (2002) *Supervision in Social Work*. New York: Columbia University Press.

Kearney, K.S. and Hyle, A.E. (2004) Drawing out emotions: The use of participant-produced drawings in qualitative inquiry, *Qualitative Research*, 4(3):361–82.

Kemmis, S. (2010) What is to be done? The place of action research, *Educational Action Research*, 18(4): 417–27. DOI: 10.1080/09650792.2010.524745

Kettle, M., McCusker, P., Shanks, L. et al. (2016) *Integrated Learning in Social Work: A review of approaches to integrated learning for social work education and practice*, Glasgow: Caledonian University. Available at: https://www.sssc.uk.com/knowledge-base/article/KA-01739/en-us (accessed 26 May 2023).

Larkin, M., Watts, S. and Clifton, E. (2006) Giving voice and making sense in interpretative phenomenological analysis, *Qualitative Research in Psychology*, 3(2): 102–20.

Merleau-Ponty, M. (1945 [2002]) *Phenomenology of Perception*. New York: Routledge.

Miller, W.R. and Rollnick, S. (2013) *Motivational Interviewing: Helping People to Change*, 3rd edn. New York: Guilford Press.

Matthews, S. (2013) Drawing as a research method: Exploring the role and experiences of Approved Mental Health Professionals, *Sage Research Methods Online* ISBN 9781446373050.

McAteer, M. (2013) *Action Research in Education*. London: Sage.

McGarvey-Gill (2023) Practice education: Boundaries of knowledge, theory and practice, in J. Hemmington and S. Vicary, S. (eds) (2023) *Making Decisions in Compulsory Mental Health Work*. Bristol: Policy Press.

Morrison, T. (2001) *Staff Supervision in Social Care: Making a Real Difference for Staff and Service Users*. Brighton: Pavilion.

Morrison, T. (2005) *Staff Supervision in Social Care*. Brighton: Pavilion.

Padgett, D. (1998a) *Qualitative Methods in Social Work Research: Challenges and Rewards*. London: Sage.

Padgett. D. (1998b) Does the glove really fit? Qualitative research and clinical social work, *Social Work*, 43(4): 373–81.

Paley, J. (2017) *Phenomenology as Qualitative Research: A Critical Analysis of Meaning Attribution*. New York: Routledge.

Poland, B.D. (1995) Transcription as an aspect of rigor in qualitative research, *Qualitative Inquiry*, 1(3): 290–310.

Puddephatt, J. (2006) Special: An interview with Kathy Charmaz: On constructing grounded theory, *Qualitative Sociology Review*, 2(3): 5–20.

Rawls, A.W. (2002) Editor's introduction, in H. Garfinkel, *Ethnomethodology's Program: Working Out Durkheim's Aphorism*. Lanham, MA: Roman and Littlefield.

Reed, M. (2018) *The Research Impact Handbook*, 2nd edn. Huntly, Scotland: Fast Track Impact Ltd.

Reid, K., Flowers, P. and Larkin, M. (2005) Exploring lived experience, *The Psychologist*, 18(1): 20–23.

Riessman, C.K. (2008) *Narrative Methods for the Human Sciences*. Thousand Oaks, CA: Sage.

Roller, M. (2015) Qualitative Research Design: Selected Articles, in *Research Design Review*. Available at http://rollerresearch.com/publications.html (accessed 26 May 2023).

Ross, L.E. (2017) An account from the inside: Examining the emotional impact of qualitative research through the lens of 'insider' research, *Qualitative Psychology*, 4(3): 326–37.

Sarantakos, S. (1993) *Social Research*. Brisbane: MacMillan Education Australia.

Shaw, I. (2018) *Research and the Social Work Picture*. Bristol: Policy Press.

Shaw, I. and Holland, S. (2014) *Doing Qualitative Research in Social Work*. London: Sage.

Shaw, I. and Lunt, N. (2018) Forms of practitioner research, *British Journal of Social Work*, 48(1): 141–57.

Shaw, R. (2011) The future's bright: Celebrating its achievements and preparing for the challenges ahead in IPA research, *Health Psychology Review*, 5(1): 28–33.

Sheldon, B. (2001) The validity of evidence-based practice in social work: A reply to Stephen Webb, *British Journal of Social Work*, 33(5): 801–809.

Shinebourne, P. (2011) The theoretical underpinning of interpretative phenomenological analysis (IPA), *Existential Analysis*, 22(1): 16–30.

Smith, J.A. (1996) Beyond the divide between cognition and discourse: Using interpretative phenomenological analysis in health psychology, *Psychology and Health*, 11(2): 261–71.

Smith, J.A. (2004) Reflecting on the development of interpretative phenomenological analysis and its contribution to qualitative psychology, *Qualitative Research in Psychology*, 1(1): 39–54.

Smith, J.A. (2007) Hermeneutics, human sciences and health: Linking theory and practice, *International Journal of Qualitative Studies on Health and Well-being*, 2(1): 3–11.

Smith, J.A. (2010) Interpretative Phenomenological Analysis: A reply to Amedeo Giorgi, *Existential Analysis*, 21(2): 186–192.

Smith, J.A. (2011a) Evaluating the contribution of interpretative phenomenological analysis, *Health Psychology Review*, 5(1): 9–27.

Smith, J.A. (2011b) Evaluating the contribution of interpretative phenomenological analysis: A reply to the commentaries and further development of criteria, *Health Psychology Review*, 5(1): 55–61.

Smith, J.A. (2011c) 'We could be diving for pearls': The value of the gem in experiential qualitative psychology, *Qualitative Methods in Psychology Bulletin*, 12: 6–15.

Smith, J.A. and Osborn, M. (2003) Interpretative Phenomenological Analysis in J.A. Smith (ed.) *Qualitative Psychology: A Practical Guide to Methods*. London: Sage.

Smith, J.A., Flowers, P. and Larkin, M. (2009) *Interpretative Phenomenological Analysis: Theory, Method and Research*. London: Sage.

Smith, J.A., Flowers, P. and Larkin, M. (2022) *Interpretative Phenomenological Analysis: Theory, Method and Research*, 2nd edn. London: Sage.

Smith J. and Nizza, I.E. (2022) *Essentials of Interpretative Phenomenological Analysis*. Washington, DC: American Psychological Association.

Starks, H. and Trinidad, S.B. (2007) Choose your method: A comparison of Phenomenology, Discourse Analysis, and Grounded Theory, *Qualitative Health Research*, 17(10): 1372–1380.

Strauss, A. and Corbin, J. (1990) *Basics of Qualitative Research: Grounded Theory Procedures and Techniques*. London: Sage.

Stutchbury, K. and Fox, A. (2009) Ethics in educational research: Introducing a methodological tool for effective ethical analysis, *Cambridge Journal of Education*, 39(4): 489–504.

Susman, G.I. and Evered, R.D. (1978) An assessment of the scientific merits of action research, *Administrative Science Quarterly*, 23(4): 582–603.

Theron, L., Mitchell, C., Smith, A. and Stuart, J. (2011) *Picturing Research: Drawing as Visual Methodology*. Rotterdam, Netherlands: Sense.

Todorova, I. (2011) Explorations with interpretative phenomenological analysis in different socio-cultural contexts. Commentary on J. Smith: Evaluating the contribution of interpretative phenomenological analysis, *Health Psychology Review*, 5(1): 34–38.

Todres, L. (2007) *Embodied Enquiry: Phenomenological Touchstones for Research, Psychotherapy and Spirituality*. London: Palgrave Macmillan.

Tsui, M. (2005) *Social Work Supervision: Context and Concepts*. London: Sage.

Vagle, M. (2018) *Crafting Phenomenological Research*, 2nd edn. New York: Routledge.

Van Manen, M. (2014) *Phenomenology of Practice*. London: Routledge.

Van Manen, M. (2016) *Researching Lived Experience: Human Science for an Action Sensitive Pedagogy*, 2nd edn. Oxford: Routledge.

Vicary, S. (2017) An Interpretative Phenomenological Analysis of the Impact of Professional Background on Role Fulfilment: A study of approved mental health practice. PhD thesis University of Manchester. Available at https://research.manchester.ac.uk/en/studentTheses/an-interpretative-phenomenological-analysis-of-the-impact-of-prof (accessed 26 May 2023).

Vicary, S. (2021) 'Pull;' the active use of dissonance. An IPA pearl to show emotion management in action, *Practice: Social Work in Action*, 33(4): 253–70.

Vicary, S., Young, A. and Hicks, S. (2017) A reflective journal as learning process and contribution to quality and validity in Interpretative Phenomenological Analysis, *Qualitative Social Work*, 16(4): 550–65.

Vicary, S., Young, A. and Hicks, S. (2019) 'Role over' or roll over? Dirty work, shift, and Mental Health Act Assessments, *British Journal of Social Work*, 9(8): 2178–206.

Webb, S. (2001) Some considerations on the validity of evidence-based practice in social work, *British Journal of Social Work*, 31(5): 57–79.

Webb, S. (2002) Evidence-based practice and decision analysis in social work, *Journal of Social Work*, 2(1): 45–63.

Weiss, R.S. (1994) *Learning from Strangers: The Art and Method of Qualitative Interview Studies*. New York: Free Press.

Wiles, F. and Vicary, S. (2019) Picturing social work, puzzles and passion: Exploring and developing transnational professional identities, *Social Work Education: The International Journal*, 38(1): 47–62.

Willig, C. (2001) *Introducing Qualitative Research in Psychology: Adventures in Theory*. Maidenhead: Open University Press.

Yardley, L. (2000) Dilemmas in qualitative health research, *Psychology and Health*, 15(2): 215–28.

Index